MYSTERIOUS
CORNWALL

Mysterious Cornwall is part of the Breedon Books *Mysterious Counties* series.

The book concentrates on all aspects of the supernatural, paranormal and mysterious in the county of Cornwall. Ghosts, myths, legends, big cats, witchcraft, sacred wells and the little people all feature. The book is arranged by subject, though each and every area of Cornwall is covered to give a wide geographical spread around the county. Instructions on finding each mysterious place are given, the event or legend associated with it is explained and a guide to what there is to see there today is included.

The book is aimed at the general reader interested in the county or in mysterious and bizarre events. The text is written in a lively, chatty style. The inclusion of numerous photos and other illustrative material adds to the appeal of this volume.

Among the mysterious places to feature are:

BOTATHAN – The road out of the village is haunted by Dorothy Dingle, who died a mysterious death in 1665. No murderer was ever caught and her ghost returns frequently.

HINGSTON DOWN – A fabulous treasure is said to be buried somewhere on this hill, guarded by the little people and accessible only to certain humans under the strangest conditions.

CALLINGTON – The waters drawn from Dupath Well, housed in a small stone shrine, are said to cure whooping cough.

TINTAGEL – The romantic ruined castle set high on a promontory overlooking the sea is the focus of numerous legends, most famously those about King Arthur and Merlin.

RUPERT MATTHEWS is a noted author on folklore, ghosts and other aspects of that parallel universe that sometimes intrudes on our own. Rupert has spent a lifetime investigating the paranormal and the bizarre. He has written over 100 books for adults and children including *Haunted Places of Devon*, *Haunted Places of Kent* and *The GhostHunter's Guide to England* (all Countryside Books).

MYSTERIOUS CORNWALL

Rupert Matthews

First published in Great Britain in 2008 by
The Breedon Books Publishing Company Limited
Breedon House, 3 The Parker Centre,
Derby, DE21 4SZ.

This paperback edition published in Great Britain in 2013 by DB Publishing,
an imprint of JMD Media Ltd

ISBN 978-1-78091-306-3

Printed and bound in the UK by Copytech (UK) Ltd Peterborough

CONTENTS

INTRODUCTION

There can be no doubt that Cornwall is a unique and beautiful part of Britain. The county is dominated by the granite mass that lies beneath the soils. It is that granite that has allowed this long, thin peninsula to withstand the pounding of the Atlantic storms as they sweep in from the west. It is that granite that forms the bedrock on which the landscape is built.

Whether it is the heights of Bodmin Moor or the cliffs of Land's End, the ancient rocks of Cornwall underlie its distinctive landscape. Nowhere else in Britain are the fields so small, so that the hedges and walls can shelter the crops from the prevailing winds that force the trees to grow with a slant to the east. Nowhere else do the stone villages huddle around ancient churches quite so closely. Nowhere else do so many tiny harbours shelter boats and yachts under the shadow of ancient farming villages.

There is also nowhere else with quite such an astonishing array of the mysterious, paranormal and downright odd. Other counties have their ghosts, their witches and their legends – but Cornwall has the lot and in numbers that seem to defy belief. It seems that almost everywhere you turn there is another mystery to be found, unearthed and studied, to the bafflement and wonder of all.

In part this may be because the tourist trade is so important to the Cornish that every story or tale is remembered and passed on to impress visitors so that they linger long enough to buy tea or lunch, or even to stay for a night or two. But there is probably more to it than that.

There is definitely something different about Cornwall. The tourist or traveller is aware of it as soon as they cross the River Tamar. Pubs, houses and boats fly the white cross on black that is the flag of St Piran, patron saint of Cornwall. East of the Tamar the flags are the red cross on white of St George of England. Not so in Cornwall. This indicates the fact that for centuries Cornwall was a distinct kingdom that stood independent of the English. Long after Cornwall became a county of England, native Cornish laws and the native Cornish language held sway here.

Indeed, Cornish as a living, working language survived until very recently. It is generally thought that the last Cornish speaker who could speak no English was the Mousehole resident Dolly Pentreath, who died in 1777. John Davey, who died in 1890, should be considered the last traditional speaker, though Alison Treganning, who died in 1906, was probably fluent in the language. By that time Robert Morton Nance was hard at work studying the Cornish language and in 1929 published *Cornish For All*, followed in 1931 by *Lessons in Spoken Cornish*. Today the language crops up quite often in names and on signs. It is taught in schools so that Cornish children can read old literature in the original and study historic documents. It is slowly reviving as a spoken language, though English remains the mother tongue of Cornwall.

The survival of the language, a form of Celtic closely related to that spoken in Brittany and, to a lesser extent, Welsh, points to the underlying cultural identity of Cornwall. This is decidedly Celtic, though the English have had a strong influence for centuries. This leaves its mark in the mysteries of Cornwall. Traditional beliefs and stories are more akin to those of Wales or Ireland than England. This makes the county something of a foreign place for some English visitors. That said I must thank the many Cornish people who have helped me in this work. Too many to mention have happily told me old stories, shown me around haunted buildings or simply pointed me on my way when I was trying to find one of the more obscure locations.

Cornwall is not exclusively Celtic. It is Cornish. In the pages of this book you will encounter some famous and some less well-known stories. They mark out Cornwall as being a special place. A wonderful place.

A mysterious place.

Chapter I

Mysterious Giants and Devils

'There were giants in the Earth in those days',
says the book of *Genesis* when talking about
those distant days before Noah's flood.

Modern scientists may scoff, but there are still those in Cornwall who are in no doubt. If they are to be believed then the county was once home to more giants than any other place in England. As for the Devil, he is held to have been very active in Cornwall in days gone by. Outsiders might suggest that Cornwall was a favourite destination of his due to the wickedness of the local people. Cornish residents would no doubt counter that the Devil had to come to the county so often for precisely the opposite reason – he had to work doubly hard in order to tempt the good Cornish folk away from the paths of righteousness.

Either way both giants and devils have been frequent visitors to Cornwall.

Take for instance the strange earthworks of Bolster Bank, just outside St Agnes on the north coast. The bank is a long ditch with the spoil thrown up to one side. On the hill behind it are three large stone cairns. According to local legend, this area was once owned by a giant named Bolster. When St Agnes brought Christianity to the area and asked Bolster for land on which to build a church, she was met with a grumpy reply. The giant told her that she could have as much land as she could clear of stones and boulders in three journeys.

St Agnes went to work, using her apron to hold the stones as she picked them up. Miraculously her apron expanded to hold a huge amount of debris. Three times she emptied her apron on top of the hill, on each occasion dumping enough rocks to create one of the cairns. She thus cleared enough land for a church and for a holy community of Christians.

Six miles away stands the prehistoric fortress of Carn Brea, within which stands a much smaller mediaeval castle. This ancient fort is said to have been the home of a giant named John Gaunt, who had a feud with Bolster. The giants passed the time by chucking stones at one another. One stone struck John Gaunt on the head and killed him, whereupon Bolster hurled more stones to bury the body of his enemy. All that was left above ground was one of John Gaunt's hands. This hand, it is said, has now turned to stone. There is a granite boulder at the western end of the fort that is shaped like a hand.

Once John Gaunt was out of the way, Bolster took to striding around his lands and those of his neighbours. One day he stopped to drink at St Agnes's Well at Chapel Porth. As he bent down he left his thumbprint on the rocks – and a curious rock formation can be seen there today as proof of the story.

Bolster had meanwhile fallen in love with St Agnes. As a devout Christian lady she wanted nothing to do with a pagan giant and brushed off his attentions. The giant Bolster was not so easily dismissed and he became such a nuisance that the Christian community begged St Agnes to do something. She accordingly went to see Bolster and promised to marry him if he would first fill up a hole in the cliff at Chapel Porth with his blood. Bolster strode over, put his arm over the hold and opened up a vein. The blood poured out, but St Agnes had tricked the giant by choosing a hole that connected down to the sea. The giant's blood flowed away. Eventually Bolster died from loss of blood. His body fell into the sea and was washed away.

Exactly the same tale is told of the anonymous giant of Dodman Point. This giant was said to have built and lived in the prehistoric fort that crowns the summit of the hill. He was a real terror, stealing livestock and crops to satisfy his awesome appetite. One day he fell ill and sent for a doctor from Gorran. Why the giant decided to trust a human doctor is unclear, but he was obviously unwise to do so. The doctor prescribed bleeding as a cure and used a sinkhole as a basin. When the giant was weak from loss of blood, the good doctor pushed him into the sea to drown.

Even more bloodthirsty was the giant known as Wrath of Portreath. He lived in a cave in the cliffs. When he was hungry he would hurl great boulders at any passing fishing boats that came too close. The giant would then wade out to club the struggling fishermen to death. The lean, skinny ones he threw back into the sea, but any plump ones he took back to his lair to eat as his supper.

Wrath met his end when the roof of his cave fell in and crushed him. The old cave can still be seen as a narrow gorge known as Ralph's Cupboard. The rocks that he used to throw at passing ships are revealed at low tide as a dangerous reef running out to sea from the cliffs. No doubt many a boat came to grief here, and the giant got the blame.

Another giant with an equally unpleasant appetite once lived at Carminowe. He had the decidedly gory habit of breaking into the churchyard to dig up and devour freshly buried corpses. The villagers tried everything they could think of. The giant was too strong to fight, so they dug pits covered with grass to trap him, but the giant avoided them. Finally the villagers abandoned their church and built a new one at St Mawgen in Meneage to serve both villages.

West along the coast on the hills above Zennor stands Carn Galver, a great hill that was once home to a gentle giant. The giant of Carn Galver enjoyed nothing better than to play hide and seek or similarly childish games with the humans who lived nearby. His favourite playmate was a young man from Choon who would walk up to the hills whenever he could find the time.

Looe was formerly home to a giant who dug a great ditch that runs seven miles inland.

One day the giant and the youngster had enjoyed a long day's play when the man said he had to go home. He turned to go and the giant tapped him on the head, saying 'Be sure to come again tomorrow, my son, and we will have a capital game.' But the giant did not know his own strength. What he thought a gentle tap was enough to crush the man's skull and his playmate fell down dead.

'Oh my son, my son,' wailed the giant. 'Why did they not make the shell of thy noddle stronger. It is as soft as a piecrust, dough-baked and made too thin by the half. How shall I ever pass the time without thee to play with.' The giant took to sitting alone on Carn Galver, gazing out sadly across the landscape. He died of a broken heart soon after.

The giant of Looe knew what to do with his time. He dug a great ditch that runs seven miles from Lerryn to Looe. It is known now as the Giant's Hedge because of the bushes that grow along it. In places it stands around 15ft tall. A local ditty runs:

'Jack the Giant had nothing to do
So he made a hedge from Lerryn to Looe.'

Another giant lived near Ludgvan, up on Trencrom Hill. He seems to have been a peaceful soul, as no stories of his misbehaviour have survived. The mounds of earth on top of the hill are said to mark his grave.

The giants who lived west of Penzance were ruled over by the giant king of Treryn Dinas, a prehistoric fortress. The giant king was said to have built Treryn Dinas in a single night, hauling it up out of the sea by magical means. He had a beautiful giantess as a wife, but she

Trencrom Hill, above Ludgvan, is marked by an earthen bank where a giant lies buried.

was unfaithful to him and fell in love with a handsome young giant from Logan. One night, as the giant king lay sleeping, the young lover crept up and stabbed him to death before throwing the body off the cliffs of Treryn into the sea. The young giant then married the giantess and became king in his place.

East of Penzance, and therefore free of the rule of the murderous giant king and his new wife, lived the giant of St Michael's Mount. This was long before the place was taken over by Christians and dedicated to St Michael. This giant married the sister of the giant of Trencrom, who lived inside the ancient fortress that crowns that hill.

The brothers-in-law got on well and, as luck would have it, were both cobblers. They were poor and had only one hammer between the two of them. This was no problem as, being giants, they could hurl the hammer to each other depending on who needed it at the time. One day the wife of the giant of St Michael's Mount happened to step out of her house and right into the path of the hammer as it was hurled from Trencrom. The hammer hit her between the eyes and killed her instantly. Both husband and brother were grief-stricken and died soon after.

The giants of the Isles of Scilly survived longer than those of Cornwall. Giants lived on Buzza's Hill, but the last of all inhabited Giant's Castle on St Mary's. They had gone by 1756 when the antiquarian William Borlase visited, but the local folk remembered them still.

It is difficult to know quite what lies behind this firm insistence that giants once strode across Cornwall. As can be seen, the giants are generally hostile to mankind and to

Christianity in particular. Although they are phenomenally strong, they are not terribly bright and can be overcome by humans who use a bit of thought. Some of these stories are clearly little more than folklore. It is possible, however, that truth lurks behind some of them. The story of Bolster and St Agnes, for instance, may refer to a pagan landowner who was persuaded to hand over land to the new religion.

The 'giant's hedge' that runs from Lerryn to Looe has been reckoned by archaeologists to date from about the sixth century. It was presumably a defensive work, which cut off the peninsula between the rivers Looe and Fowey from the rest of Cornwall. Who built it and why is now unknown. Perhaps this nameless giant was invented to explain the inexplicable.

Some think that this belief in giants is a garbled folk memory of a time when there really was a race of humans living in Britain that were bigger and stronger, but not quite so intelligent, as ourselves. Science knows these people as the Neanderthals, an extinct side branch of human evolution. These Neanderthals lived in Europe for hundreds of thousands of years before modern humans began arriving. The two species of humans lived side by side for thousands of years. So far as is known the most recent Neanderthal bones date to around 30,000 years ago, but some isolated populations may have survived much longer. No one knows when they finally died out nor what tales of them were remembered by our own ancestors.

It is interesting to note what happened to William Borlase in 1752. Borlase was a gentleman with an interest in antiquities – effectively an early amateur archaeologist. He was excavating some ancient burial mounds when a terrible storm suddenly broke, lashing the landscape with wind and hail for some hours. Next day, the local farmers blocked his return to the excavations. They told him that the digging had upset the giants who were buried in the mounds, and that this had caused the storm. Clearly giants were not only firmly believed in as recently as 1752, but they were held to have supernatural powers.

Those powers were as nothing compared to those that could be wielded by the Devil himself.

When the Devil comes to Cornwall, he invariably starts his visit at Carn Kenidzhek. From this high, isolated point he can gaze out over the landscape to spy out evildoers. It is said that two miners were walking past Carn Kenidzhek as night drew in late one evening, when they were overtaken by a tall, dark-haired man riding a spirited black stallion and dressed all in black velvet.

'Where are you going?' asked one miner.

'Up to the cairn to see the wrestling,' replied the expensively dressed stranger. 'Come along.'

The miners followed and found themselves confronted by a crowd of demons, two of whom were stripped to the waist and ready to wrestle. When the horseman leapt down from his mount he threw off his cloak to reveal that he was the Devil himself. The miners cowered

*St Michael's Mount was home to a giant
who left after his wife came to a tragic end.*

back but were unable to flee. A terrific wrestling match followed, which ended with one demon being so badly injured that he seemed to be dying. Acting without thinking, one of the miners said a prayer for the dying. At once the demon host rose screaming into the air as an earthquake struck and total darkness came down.

The terrified miners flung themselves to the ground and did not look up until silence returned. They found themselves alone, but utterly bewildered. They could not find their way home and wandered aimlessly until dawn. Then they found themselves back at Carn Kenidzhek. The granite tor here is of a particularly weird shape. When a strong wind blows it emits a haunting, howling noise. It is for this reason that it got its name, which means in Cornish 'the hooting tor'.

That the Devil is fond of wrestling when he visits Cornwall is shown by a story from Ladock. Young Jacky Trevail of Ladock was the champion wrestler of the village back in the 18th century. One day he came home with a magnificent gold-laced hat that he had won as a prize in a wrestling competition and headed down to the pub to celebrate. Jacky celebrated long and hard, boasting 'I am open to challenge by any man living – and I wouldn't mind a bout with the Devil himself'. As he weaved out of the pub and passed the church on his way home Jacky was met by a well-dressed stranger. The newcomer admired the hat and offered to match it by a wager of five guineas if Jacky Trevail would return to wrestle with him at midnight the following night. Jacky agreed.

Next day, Jacky began to worry. He became concerned that the stranger might indeed by the Devil that he had challenged when drinking at the pub. He hurried to Ladock Church to consult Parson Wood. Wood shared Jacky's concerns, but told him not to worry. If the stranger were a man Jacky could beat him, but if he were Devil then Parson Wood could beat him. Wood gave Jacky a page torn from a Bible and covered with arcane symbols and told him to put it in his waistcoat pocket.

Next night, as midnight drew on, Jacky arrived outside the churchyard to meet his opponent. The stranger duly arrived and the two fell to wrestling. It was a close match, but after some minutes the stranger managed to get Jacky off the ground. It seemed the contest was all but over, but then the stranger's hand touched Jacky's waistcoat. With a scream of agony the stranger dropped Jacky.

'You have some concealed weapon about ye that has wounded me,' accused the stranger. 'Take off that waistcoat and let us begin again.' Jacky refused to take off the waistcoat, now convinced that he was dealing with no human wrestler. After another bout of grappling, the stranger broke off the combat again. 'Parson Wood is here,' he said. 'I can feel his eyes upon me.'

Jacky Trevail pounced, and he threw the stranger on to his back. The stranger cursed savagely, sprouted great black wings and soared up into the sky belching flames and smoke. The Devil, for it was clearly he, flew off toward St Enoder. Parson Wood emerged from the

The Angel Hotel at Helston contains the Hell Stone from which the town is named.

church to congratulate Jacky on his victory. Jacky was under few illusions and knew it was only because of Parson Wood's piece of paper that he was not even then on his way to Hell. The young man remained the wrestling champion of the area, but he never again drank to excess nor called on the Devil for a wager.

The Devil had rather more luck when he visited Towednack. For some reason he took against the pinnacles and battlements that crowned the church tower, as they do the towers of so many churches in Cornwall. The evil one stole them away. The vicar called on some local builders, who replaced them. The Devil knocked them down. The builders replaced them. The Devil smashed them to pieces. This time the builders gave up, and so Towednack Church stands without pinnacles or battlements to this day.

The Angel Hotel at Helston, on the other hand, contains a stone that the Devil left behind. It used to stand in the courtyard, but building works in the early 20th century meant that it now lies under the floor. This granite boulder was formerly the gate of hell itself. The Devil was struggling with St Michael the Archangel in the skies over Helston when he dropped the stone. Nobody has ever had the courage to move it since. The name of Helston is derived from Hell Stone, or so it is said.

The Devil had no luck at all the day he came to Tolcarne in 1592, but the story does point to a possible origin for all these tales of demonic activity. He came, apparently, to steal fishermen's nets. Before he could begin his evil work, the Devil was confronted by the vicar and the church choir, who were gathered for hymn practice. The vicar chased the Devil so fast that the Devil tripped and fell. As he picked himself up the Devil turned to glare at the vicar and choir. He shouted out 'Buckah, Buckah, Buckah', then sprang into the air and flew off. A terrific storm then came down to lash Tolcarne.

The word 'Buckah' is almost certainly derived from 'Pwca', the name of a pre-Christian sky god. It would seem that the story, although said to have taken place in 1592, actually refers to the Christian mission that converted this area of Cornwall. That event probably happened sometime between 350 and 550 – dates from this period of history are notoriously tricky to pin down with any accuracy.

It was the habit of the early Christians to denounce pagan gods as demons sent by the Devil to lead men astray. Thus Pwca the sky god was, to the missionaries, the Devil. The story may relate back to the way that the worship of Pwca was driven out by the Christian faith. In its turn this may explain why the Devil seems to have visited Cornwall so often – he didn't, but the old gods did.

Chapter 2

Mysterious Piskies

West of the River Parrett there are no fairies to be found, but there are plenty of piskies – or pixies, to give them their more familiar Somerset name. These little people are generally held to be a distinct type of entity from the fairies. Indeed, according to at least one old Cornish legend, they are enemies of the fairies and agreed on the Parrett as the border between their lands only after a long and bitter war.

Be that as it may, the piskies are deeply embedded in the Cornish countryside. There are many places that are said to be their particular home and many stories are told of encounters between them and humans. These piskies are not thought to be downright hostile to humans, but they clearly are not especially well disposed toward us. One of the favourite tricks is to play a prank on travelling humans and so make them piskie-led.

This rather disturbing experience will come without warning and may strike when in familiar surroundings or when passing through strange territory. At its most simple the traveller will be unable to see a road or path, even though it is in plain view. Even today it is possible to drive up and down the same stretch of main road looking for a lane leading to a village and be quite unable to find it – then to return next day and find it at once. There would seem to be only one sure cure for being piskie-led. That is to turn your coat inside out and put it back on that way. Some suggest carrying a piece of iron about your person, or having some bread in your pocket, but this does not always seem to work.

In 1923 a woman named Mrs Hamilton was walking from her home in Tresahor to visit a friend in Constantine. She knew the path well, having walked it a hundred times previously. This time, however, she climbed a stile into a field and at once got piskie-led. No matter how hard she tried she could not find the stile out the other side. Returning the way she had come she could not find the stile by which she had entered the field either, nor was any gate to be seen. She walked around the field three times, finding only blank and impassable hedges on all sides. After an hour or so of this, the woman heard a farmer working nearby and called out for help. At once the spell was broken and she could see the various stiles and gates in their usual positions.

More dangerously, those who are piskie-led may find themselves being lured into serious danger. More than one walker has been treading what seemed to be a broad, firm path, only to snap suddenly out of some kind of reverie to find themselves alone on a lonely stretch of moorland surrounded by treacherous bogs. Other walkers vanish completely and are never seen again, having perished due to exposure on the high moorlands. Some people believe that those who are piskie-led in this way have offended the piskies without realising it.

The Merry Maidens stone circle near Boleigh is a well-known haunt of the piskies.

The outer ramparts of Castle Dinas, within which the piskies are said to hold a regular fair.

Conversely, the piskies will go out of their way to help those humans whom they like, or who have done them a favour. Being on the side of the piskies can be a major advantage in Cornwall.

There are different versions of what the piskies actually look like, partly because so few people ever see them. Some say that they are almost the size of a human and could be mistaken for one, while others say that they are only about 3ft or so tall. Either way, the piskies are said to be very fond of wild plants and of areas not subjected to ploughing. They usually wear green clothes and have round faces as well as, according to some, sporting red hair and turned up noses.

Among the places beloved by the piskies is the ancient burial barrow at Ballowal, near St Just. On moonlit nights the piskies gather here to dance to their beautifully haunting music. The Cheesewring, a prehistoric megalith on Bodmin Moor, was another haunt of the piskies, as was the Merry Maidens stone circle near Boleigh. Castle Dinas is the place where the piskies gather for a fair.

They also like to frequent the area around Madron, or at least they did in the 18th century when the place was famous for them. In the early 20th century Hayle became known as something of a focus for piskie activity. At least one local man habitually left out a saucer of milk for them at night. The piskies of Bone, near Penzance, were more willing to enter into trade. If coins were left for them on an ancient standing stone near the village they would take them away, leaving in return gifts of various kinds.

The Gump, a stretch of common near Sennen, was thought to be the site of the Piskie Fair where the Cornish piskies gathered to buy and sell their goods. It is said that an old man from Sennen once tried to push his way into the Piskie Fair, intent on stealing some valuable item that he could sell for cash in Penzance. The piskies, of course, saw him coming and struck him on the nose. He was immediately paralysed, being unable to move for hours.

The hills of Lady Downs between Zennor and Ludgvan were well known to be a haunt of the piskies, but this did not stop a young woman named Cherry, from Zennor, falling foul of them. Young Cherry could find no work in her village, so one spring she set off for the hiring fair at Ludgvan to look for work in domestic service. She was walking over Lady Downs when at a crossroads she met a finely dressed gentleman riding toward Ludgvan.

The man asked Cherry where she was bound and, on being told she was seeking a position, told her that he was heading for Ludgvan to hire a girl servant. He was seeking somebody to look after his young son, for he was a widower himself and was busy with his business. Cherry accepted, and the gentleman turned back the way he had come to lead the girl back to his house.

The route the pair took was, at first, familiar to Cherry. But soon they began to go down lanes and past landmarks that she did not recognise, although she had often passed this way. Finally they came to a deep ravine that had set in it a fine mansion. The gentleman led

A tor on the Lady Downs, close to the spot where a girl from Zennor had a famous encounter with the piskies.

Cherry in, showing her the nursery where his son lived and the kitchens where she was to prepare his meals. The gentleman told Cherry that his son had weak eyesight and that she was to put some ointment, which he gave her, into his eyes each morning.

Cherry was happy in her new job. The gentleman treated her well, while the other servants were kind and helpful. The boy was a good learner and behaved in a polite fashion. Cherry's only real problem was that she was forbidden to leave the house and gardens, even for a day. She missed her family and friends, but time passed well enough.

Cherry could not help noticing that her charge's eyes became bright and sparkling each morning after she rubbed the ointment into them. One day she decided to try the ointment on herself. She had barely touched one eye with the paste when it began to sting with an intense pain. She hurriedly washed the eye clear, but realised that something very odd had happened. Out of the corner of the eye that the ointment had touched she could see a rather different place from that which she could see otherwise.

The mansion was grand enough, but the gardens were dark and filled a vast cavern that had no sunlight. The boy that she was caring for was no longer a young human, but a piskie. All the servants were likewise piskies. When the fine gentleman came home that evening, Cherry saw that he too was a piskie and he quickly realised that she could see the truth.

The piskie master told Cherry that she could not stay as a servant now that she had used the ointment and could see the truth. He led her out of the mansion, through the cavern and into passageways that led up through the rock to the surface above until they reached the crossroads on Lady Downs. There he paid young Cherry her wages and sent her on her way. Thereafter, Cherry had the gift of seeing the piskies out of the corner of her eye, even when they had disguised themselves as animals.

In 1846 the *Cornish Reporter* newspaper carried a story about a pony from Lostwithiel that had fallen victim to another of the piskies' favourite tricks. The farmer who owned the pony found it one morning lying in a corner of its field in a dreadful state. He sent for the local farrier, who had some skills as a vet. By the time the farrier arrived the pony was better, but it was ill again next morning. This time the farrier arrived quickly enough to see the sickness. He became convinced that the pony had been ridden by piskies during the night.

That evening the farrier and farmer climbed up into a tree overlooking the pony's field to see what would happen. Soon after midnight five small men appeared as if from nowhere. They fell to wrestling and, after a long series of bouts, one of them emerged victorious. The winner then leapt onto the back of the pony and dug his heels into its flanks. The horse took off at a gallop while the rider sang a series of obscene songs. For some time the pony careered around the field until, with dawn starting to break, it collapsed. The five piskies then slipped away. The farmer stabled his pony after that and, according to the *Cornish Reporter*, it suffered no further ill effects.

One evening in 1810 a tailor named William Dunn was walking home from Truro through St Kea. He was passing the churchyard when he was startled to see a group of piskies crossing the path in front of him. The little men, around 3ft tall, were all dressed alike in black hats and red jackets. They walked in single file, each taking his turn to scramble over the hedge into the churchyard. Dunn watched them pass by, seemingly rooted to the spot. As the last of them entered the churchyard, Dunn regained the use of his limbs and raced after them. Although he was only a second or two behind them, by the time he got into the churchyard they had vanished.

Piskies were seen in St Ives at around 11.30pm one night in 1877. A girl named Rebecca Noall was employed at a dressmaker's in the town and, because of an urgent order, she and the other girls were working until 11pm. Rebecca's father came to the shop at 11pm to walk her home. The two were walking down Fore Street when the father suddenly grabbed Rebecca's arm and hissed at her to stand still in perfect silence.

Walking down the street toward the pair was a group of four piskies. The little people stood about the height of Rebecca's waist and were dressed in black hats and loose cloaks. While the two humans stood still, the piskies walked past, ignoring them completely. Once the piskies were out of sight, Rebecca's father relaxed and the pair continued on their way home.

Another lady to meet the piskies was Mrs Sophie Dowrick of Philleigh, who came across them in 1927. Mrs Dowrick was one of those ladies who collected medicinal herbs to make up into infusions for the locals. She said that she met the piskies at dawn one day when she was gathering dew-covered plants in the woods. They too, she said, were gathering plants, but they fled as soon as they saw her.

In 1687 a six-year-old girl called Agnes Martin went missing from her home at St Agnes. The surrounding countryside was searched diligently and messages were sent out far and wide, but no sign of the girl was found. Then in 1690 a girl came stumbling up to a gentleman at a fair in the Midlands saying that she was from St Agnes in Cornwall and begging to be taken back home. The girl, aged around nine, was clearly in a state of some distress, so the gentleman took her home and sent a letter to the vicar at St Agnes asking advice.

A quick exchange of letters revealed the girl to be Agnes Martin. She said that she had spent the missing years as a prisoner of the piskies. She had been forced to live in a small cottage which had only two rooms. She was allowed out only at night, and then only when accompanied by the woman piskie who lived in the cottage. The cottage, Agnes said, moved about so that each time she went out she emerged in a different place. Agnes said she had been forced to perform menial household chores and had been fed on scraps and leftovers. She claimed that one day the piskie woman had left the cottage door unlocked. Agnes had slipped out to find herself at a fair, so she had gone to the best-dressed man she could find to ask for help.

It was a curious story. Agnes Martin had most certainly been missing for three years. The vicar of St Agnes believed, after questioning Agnes for some time, that he had solved the riddle. He thought that the young girl had been kidnapped by gypsies to be kept as a sort of domestic slave. The tiny cottage that moved about was, he thought, a caravan, while the piskie woman was a gypsy who had told young Agnes that she was in the hands of piskies to keep her in fear. The vicar had no proof, but it was the most convincing explanation that anyone could devise.

The closest that any visitor to Cornwall can be guaranteed to get to the piskies these days is to visit those places where they are said to congregate. The old piskie well outside Pelynt is one of these, but it is not easy to find. North of Pelynt a lane signed to Muchlarnik turns left off the B3359 at the top of a hill. This lane should be followed for a mile to reach a T-junction, then those wishing to find the well should turn left up the lane heading for Hobb Park Farm. After a few hundred yards the lane takes a sharp left turn and a layby offers parking spaces. Continue along the lane to where a flight of stone steps goes down the hillside on the right. This leads to the small cavern in which the natural spring emerges from the ground.

Inside the tiny cave is a large stone bowl carved with abstract geometric designs that might be a thousand years old, and may be much older. The water trickles out of the rock to fall into the bowl, which overflows to allow the water to run out from the cave and disappear into the soil. The little cave has been decorated with plastic fairies by somebody, and is kept clean and regularly swept out.

The entrance to the piskie well of Pelynt, a natural underground spring that the piskies protect against anyone who seeks to change it.

The piskies of Pelynt are, on the whole, friendly to humans. They have been known to help with threshing the corn and other tasks about the farm. But the piskies are not to be treated lightly, for they can exact a terrible revenge when they put their minds to it. So the wise visitor will bring a pin or other small piece of metal to leave as a gift for the piskies at St Nun's Well.

One local farmer a couple of centuries back became greedy and forgot to treat the piskies at St Nun's Well with proper respect, and he suffered for it. The farmer decided that the stone bowl that catches the spring water was just the right size to serve as a pig trough at his farm. He brought along a pair of oxen, yoked them up to the stone bowl and set them to heave. The strong oxen dragged the bowl to the farmyard, and the farmer was proud of his work.

The piskies, however, were angry. They loved St Nun's well as it was and believed they owned the ancient stone bowl. That night they rolled the bowl back to its rightful place at the well. The next day the irate farmer yoked up his oxen and again dragged the stone bowl to his farmyard, only for the piskies to return it a second time. The third day the farmer again removed the bowl, but this time the piskies had had enough. They came to the farm in numbers and not only recovered the stone bowl, but also struck the farmer raving mad and made the oxen so sick they died within the week.

There can be no doubt that the Cornish believed very firmly in piskies. Some of the stories about them are probably no more than just stories – that of Cherry of Zennor being a prime example. The experience of Agnes Martin may or may not have been down to gypsies, but certainly sounds more like a human crime that was blamed on piskies than anything else.

Other reports are more difficult to explain away. Sophie Dowrick, Rebecca Noall and William Dunn were all convinced that they had seen piskies. There is no reason to doubt that they had seen something.

In the 19th and early 20th centuries folklorists were inclined to agree with A.K. Jenkin when he wrote: 'The piskies represent a folk-memory of an ancient race of inhabitants who were conquered by the Celts on their arrival in Cornwall, but who continued for long afterwards to lead a furtive existence in the moorlands and cliffs, till finally they faded away altogether and were remembered only in old wives' tales and tradition'. The fact that so many piskie tales were linked to old standing stones and similar ancient monuments might support this idea.

It is interesting to recall that the piskies of Cornwall were said to have defeated the fairies of England in a great battle on the banks of the River Parrett, which thereafter became the border between the two races of little people. It is known that in the year 658 the advancing English fought a battle against the Celtic kingdom of Dumnonia, that then included Cornwall, Devon and much of Dorset and Somerset. The English won the battle and a new border was drawn that ran along the Parrett. Was the firmly held belief about the piskies and fairies a recollection of this ancient war and treaty?

More recently some people have been taking a fresh look at the old stories about the little people. Leaving aside the more elaborate tales, those that seem to recount genuine encounters between humans and piskies give a fairly clear image of the mysterious little people. They are said to be between 3 and 4ft tall. They have round heads, often topped by a black hat or headgear, and wear clothes that are unlike those of humans. The piskies usually appear to people who are alone or in small groups and nearly always in the evening or around dawn. The piskies seem to have the power to paralyse humans for a short period of time, or to confuse them as to where they are. There is often a reported loss of time, with people who encounter piskies arriving home much later than they should have done although they thought they were delayed by the piskies for only a minute or two.

All these features are also found in encounters between humans and a much more modern entity of equally mysterious origins. These are the little humanoids that reportedly emerge from UFOs. It is striking that modern ufonauts should behave in ways almost identical to those of the piskies of yesteryear. Some conclude that the diminutive humanoids that are being met are one and the same, but that in the 19th century they were interpreted by those who saw them as piskies, while the 21st-century witnesses interpret them as being ufonauts.

Whatever the truth, the piskies are a very real part of Cornwall, and given their apparent powers it is probably best to treat them with all due respect and courtesy. Just in case.

Chapter 3

Mysterious Mermaids

The mermaids of Cornwall are very different from those of popular imagination. The general image that most people have of a mermaid is of a beautiful if idle creature who sits about combing her hair and singing. She might seek to lure ships to dangerous rocks, but on the whole is fairly benign and more interested in looking pretty than much else. In most illustrations or animated cartoons she has the body of a woman and the tail of a fish and is often shown with a comb and mirror.

Not so the mermaids of Cornwall. These are enormously powerful water spirits who can – and do – interact with humans in a number of rather surprising ways.

By far the most famous of all the Cornish mermaids is the mermaid of Zennor. Many years ago the people of Zennor were surprised to see a stranger slip into their church, dedicated to St Senara, to sit right at the back. She was a pretty young lady dressed in a fine, long gown of exquisite workmanship. Just before the service ended the lady got up and left. When the parishioners emerged she was nowhere to be seen. For a while gossip was rife as to who the lady had been, but gradually interest waned. Those who thought of her at all assumed she had been passing on that Sunday morning and had stopped for the religious service before travelling on.

Then a month or so later she returned. Again she entered quietly, sat at the back and left as mysteriously as she had arrived. Over the coming months she came several times to attend the services at St Senara's. It became clear that she was entranced by the singing of the choir, and in particular by the voice of Matthew Trewhella. Young Trewhella was the churchwarden's son. He was a strapping young farmer who had good looks to match his fine voice.

One Sunday, after the service ended, the villagers saw Matthew Trewhella talking to the mysterious stranger on the banks of the stream that runs through the village. Not wanting to intrude on the youngsters in the early stages of what might have been a romance, the villagers kept their distance. Matthew and the stranger were seen walking along the stream, heading for Pendour Cove where it runs into the sea. They were never seen again.

For weeks the villagers wondered what had happened to their young chorister. The Trewhella family sent messages far and wide, but no sign of their son could be found. It was the talk of Cornwall.

Five months later, a fisherman came running from St Ives. He asked for the Trewhella household, then demanded to have a description of the pretty stranger who had lured young Trewhella away. He then poured out his tale. He had been fishing off the coast of Pendour Cove and had thrown out the anchor to keep his boat steady while he worked. A short while

The 'mermaid pew' in the church at Zennor commemorates the most famous of all Cornish mermaids.

later a woman's head had bobbed to the surface beside his boat. Obviously the pretty girl was a mermaid, and the fisherman grew nervous as he knew that to offend the merfolk was dangerous. But the girl smiled pleasantly enough.

'Sir,' she called out. 'Would you please lift your anchor. It is blocking the entrance to my cave and I want to get home to my dear Matty and my children.'

The description of the mermaid matched that of the mysterious stranger. Clearly Matthew Trewhella had fallen in love with a mermaid and had gone to live with her beneath the waves. The legend is commemorated by a carved pewend in the church. The carving is thought to be around 600 years old. It shows a mermaid looking out toward the viewer while holding up her mirror and her comb. It has got a bit battered over the years and is now placed in the side chapel, but it remains clear enough.

Interestingly, St Senara had a rather watery life. She was a devout Christian who was married to King Goello of Brittany sometime around the year 450, just as the Roman Empire was breaking up. Goello's mother was a pagan who deeply resented the influence that the beautiful and virtuous young Christian had on her son. When Senara became pregnant, her angry mother-in-law fabricated evidence of infidelity and had Senara nailed in a barrel and thrown into the sea. An angel appeared who cared for Senara as she gave birth, providing her with food and drink. The barrel was washed up in Ireland, where the mother and child were taken in by a fisherman and his wife. When she recovered, Senara and her son, named Budoc, set out to found churches and convert the local pagans to Christianity. After various adventures in Ireland the pair came to Cornwall, where they founded the church of St Senara among others. King Goello heard of his wife's survival and her good works. He sent men to bring her back to Brittany where she was reinstated as queen and Budoc was recognised as his heir.

So it ended happily for all concerned, except the wicked stepmother. The church of St Senara gave its name to the village, now corrupted to Zennor. The original church is thought to have stood rather closer to the sea than the one that stands today, in a field where seventh-century ruins have been excavated. The current church was begun in around 1125, extended in 1451 and restored in 1890. A stained-glass window of St Senara is to be found in the chancel.

Another mermaid came ashore on the beaches around Lizard Point. A fisherman named Lutey from the village of Cury was walking the beach at low tide, looking for whatever the sea may have thrown up, when he heard sobbing. Hurrying towards the sound, Lutey found a mermaid sitting in a tidal rock pool. The mermaid dived down to the base of the pool, but Lutey sat down and began chatting to her in friendly tones about nothing in particular.

Eventually the mermaid came up to the surface to talk to Lutey. She told him that she had come close inshore, attracted by the scent of flowers, but had become trapped in the pool when the tide had gone out. She asked Lutey to carry her back to the sea and asked him what

So he put on his most wheedling voice.

A local fisherman named Lutey met a mermaid on a beach near the Lizard. It proved to be a lucky day for him.

he wanted in return. Lutey thought. He knew that the merfolk were magical creatures quite capable of rewarding those that helped them. But he also knew that these sea people could be vengeful and were easy to offend. He did not want to appear too greedy or heartless.

'I will not wish,' said Lutey, 'for silver and gold. But give me the power to do good to my neighbours. First to break the spells of witchcraft, next to charm away diseases. And third to discover thieves and restore stolen goods.'

Sennen Cove, where mermaids have been seen perched on the rocks combing their hair in the traditional manner.

The mermaid agreed, so Lutey hoisted her in his arms and carried her down to the edge of the sea. Before she went, the mermaid gave Lutey her comb. 'Whenever you need me, comb the surf with this and I will come,' she declared. Then she dived into the waters and was gone.

It was in this way that Lutey became the most powerful wise man, or wizard, in Cornwall. He passed on his gifts and the mermaid's comb to his son, who passed them on to his son. When he visited Cury in the 19th century the folklorist Arthur Norway met a Mr Lutey who showed him the mermaid's comb as proof of the story.

The fate of the original Mr Lutey was also described to Norway. Some nine years after his encounter with the mermaid at the Lizard, Lutey was out fishing with his regular crew. As they worked on the nets, the men saw a mermaid surface a short distance off. She waved at them, then beckoned to Lutey.

'It is her', said Lutey. 'My time has come.' He then dived into the sea and was never seen again.

Among the places along the coast where mermaids are likely to be seen are Cudden Point and Sennen Cove. At both places the mermaids have been seen perched on rocks offshore, combing their hair in the traditional manner. They will dive into the waves if any boat approaches. The mermaids of Sennen Cove are linked to a mysterious patch of mist which will sometimes settle over the Cowloe Rock. The locals took the mist to be some sort of guardian spirit. It appeared only when a storm was brewing and served to warn the locals not to put to sea.

There is certainly something odd about the mist, for it forms a solid bank of fog, though all around the weather may be sunny and clear. Strange hooting noises have been heard emerging from this mist and, at night, it seems as if lanterns are moving around within it. One foolish fisherman once rowed his boat into the mist. As his fellows watched from shore, the boat was swallowed up by the mist. Then the mist dissipated, leaving behind only the rock. There was no sign of the boat nor of its owner.

A fisherman at Padstow was even more foolish. Not only did he pay with his own life for offending a mermaid, but with the lives of others. Nobody is exactly certain what happened, which only goes to show how easy it is to offend a mermaid. One day, as the fishermen from Padstow put out to sea from the estuary of the Camel, a mermaid was seen splashing about in the water. She approached the boat of this particular fisherman and seemed to talk to him. She then ducked down beneath the waves. The day's fishing went well, and all caught well. As the little fleet headed back a swell presaging a storm got up. The boat of the fisherman who had spoken to the mermaid led the way. Suddenly his boat shivered as if it had hit something and stuck fast. The swell quickly pounded the boat to pieces and the fisherman drowned. Aghast, the other fishermen proceeded carefully. They found a great sandbank had appeared off the mouth of the Camel where none had been before. Obviously the fisherman had offended the mermaid, who had thrown up the great bank in revenge. The

The village of Seaton lost its prosperity after a vengeful mermaid threw up the sandbank, seen here on the right of the photograph, that blocked access to the harbour.

treacherous sandbank is still there, lurking just beneath the waves to wreck the unwary and take more human lives.

Another huge sandbank was thrown up by the mermaids off Seaton and Downderry on the south coast, and for a similar reason. Seaton used to be a prosperous fishing port centuries ago, like Looe or Polperro. Then one day a fisherman saw a beautiful girl sitting on the a rock by the sea combing her hair. He saw her from behind and thought it was one of the village girls. Seeing that she was naked he thought it would be a prank to creep up on her. So he did. But when he touched her shoulder to surprise her, the girl turned around and it was a mermaid. She screamed at him in anger and threw shells and rocks at him, but he hit back with his knife and drew blood. The mermaid dived into the sea and began swimming back and forth across the harbour mouth. As she did so she caused the sand to bank up and block the harbour mouth, making it useless to fishermen.

Undoubtedly the popular imagery of the mermaid to be found outside Cornwall derives partly from classical legend and partly from mediaeval Christian iconography. In the second century AD, the Roman traveller Lucian described the Phoenician goddess Atargatis as having the body of a woman and the tail of a fish. She was associated with the Roman goddess of love and beauty, Venus, who was often shown admiring herself in a mirror. At some point Atargatis-Venus got confused with the Greek Sirens. These creatures were thought of as being half-woman, half-bird. They sat on rocks and tried to lure sailors to their doom with beautiful, irresistible singing.

To mediaeval Christian theologians, the mermaid was the epitome of lust. She had probably acquired this reputation by her links to the pagan goddess Venus. By 1400 at the latest the mermaid was being shown in her modern guise with fish's tail, mirror and comb. By around 1550 she had acquired a new trait, that of seeking to marry a human husband and thereby gain a soul. This gave her a new motive for seducing sailors. Victorian painters took up the image with enthusiasm, producing a number of sensuous paintings that fixed the seductive mermaid in the popular imagination.

Some have sought to find a real-life inspiration for the mermaid. Some have settled on the dugong or the manatee, both fairly inoffensive marine mammals. The dugong inhabits the coasts of the Indian Ocean, while the manatee frequents the Atlantic. The bulky, rotund 10ft-long body of these creatures may not seem much like the seductive mermaid, but they sometimes float with head and shoulders bobbing above the waves and they can look vaguely human. The fact that the females nurse their young by supporting them in their flippers and cuddling them to the chest may increase the illusion. But the link is likely to be wholly illusory. The mermaid of popular image derives not from the mistaken reports of sailors but from classical mythology and mediaeval theology.

The mermaids of Cornwall have quite different origins. As we have seen they do not sport a fish tail, but seem to be entirely human – at least when they choose to come ashore. Nor are they so preoccupied with looking beautiful as might be imagined. They are also quite clearly of great power and have a high degree of control over the seas. The inspiration behind these mermaids must be sought elsewhere than in the classical world.

The Cornish, before they were converted to Christianity, believed in a vast number of gods and goddesses. A few of these were worshipped widely among the Celtic tribes of Britain. Lug the warrior, Cernunnos of the beasts and Macha the mother were the great deities, but each village, hill or river had its own deity, and it is here that the Cornish mermaids seem to belong. Celtic water deities were generally female and powerful. The little that has survived the efforts of early Christians to destroy their memory, shows them as being both friendly and hostile to humans, and certainly capable of loving men or even of marrying them.

All these traits are found in the Cornish mermaids. It is likely that their character and appearance, perhaps even the individual stories, are derived from lost pagan tales and memories of minor goddesses. A similar origin may lie behind the terrifying phantoms to be found at St Buryan and elsewhere. Perched on a hill south west of Penzance, St Buryan offers views south to the English Channel and west to the Atlantic. On certain nights it is possible to hear the sounds of a hunting horn echoing across the skies. If so, it is as well to hide as quickly as possible. What is approaching is no ordinary hunt, but the Wild Hunt.

The hounds that lead the Wild Hunt are large and black with eyes that glow with an inner fire like red-hot coals. Their haunting baying is a sound that is eerily terrifying and, once heard, is never forgotten. Behind the hounds come the riders – huge men clad all in black and riding monstrous chargers of great power. Leading them is the terrible figure of the wild huntsman himself. He is beautifully dressed, with a pair of stag's horns on his head, and he rides the greatest horse of them all. Urging the steed on he leaps every hedge or fence with ease, pounding in the wake of the hounds. The Wild Hunt is not out after fox or stag, but after the souls of the damned.

The Wild Hunt is generally held to be the Devil and his demons riding forth from Hell to track down and catch the souls that are their due. As elsewhere, however, today's demons might be yesterday's gods. The early Christian church was in the habit of describing pagan deities as evil demons in an effort to persuade their worshippers to abandon them. One of the greatest of the Celtic pagan gods does appear to be very similar to the Wild Huntsman: Cernunnos.

Cernunnos was worshiped across the Celtic lands. Representations of him have been found in Ireland, Britain, France and northern Italy. He is usually shown dressed as a chief or king, complete with jewel encrusted gold torc around his neck. On his head Cernunnos wears a pair of stag antlers. His role was as Lord of the Beasts. He ruled over the forests and the wild animals that inhabited them. He survived the Roman conquest and continued to be a leading deity worshipped by countryfolk until the triumph of Christianity.

Cernunnos certainly sounds a good prototype for the Wild Huntsman, but in the village of St Germans they tell a quite different story. The village stands on a tongue of land which pushes out between the broad tidal flows of the Lynher and Tiddy rivers and is bypassed by

St Germans Church.

the main roads. Back in the Middle Ages, the story goes, the Augustinian Priory of St Germans was sent Dando, a new monk from Italy, and a very wicked monk he was too. He came from a wealthy family and had taken holy orders to avoid secular justice for one of his many sins.

Having arrived in St Germans, Dando saw no reason why an oath of poverty, chastity and holiness should stop his pleasures. He had brought his private money with him and spent it freely on a pack of hounds for hunting, on luxurious foods for his private rooms and on enormous quantities of drink in the local taverns. Nor was he averse to purchasing the attentions of the less respectable local girls. His debauched lifestyle would have been a disgrace to any normal young man. For a monk of holy orders, it was the scandal of the county. Retribution was, however, on Dando's heels.

One day he was out hunting with a bunch of his cronies. Luck was with Dando and he caught a fine stag just before noon. The huntsmen called a halt for lunch, which Dando attacked with his customary vigour and called for ale. Nobody had brought any because it was Sunday and Dando fell into a rage.

'Damn your Sabbath Day,' Dando yelled. 'Someone fetch me some ale'.

At that moment another hunter appeared, dressed all in black and leading a pack of black hounds. He pulled up alongside Dando and leaned down to offer a large flask filled with ale.

'Had much luck with your hunting?' asked Dando, pointing to his own stag.

'Not until now,' declared the stranger. He grabbed Dando by his collar and hauled him up on to the saddle bow and galloped off. Followed by his great, black hounds, the stranger rode straight in to the River Lynher, where the waters closed over him, his hounds and the sacrilegious Dando in a boiling confusion from which steam and fire erupted.

It was not long before Dando came back from the Hell to which he had condemned himself. This time he led the pack of great black hounds as they raced over the Cornish countryside. But he did not hunt stags or deer. Not any more. Now Dando was the leader of the Wild Hunt, and he was after the souls of the damned to take back to his master the Devil.

Better disposed to humans than the Wild Hunt, but just as ambivalent as the mermaids, were the knockers. These folk lived deep underground and were encountered in the tin mines, back in the days before heavy machinery. They were usually heard rather than seen. When miners heard the sounds of pickaxes at work coming out of solid rock, then they knew that the knockers were at work on a rich seam of tin somewhere nearby. The knockers were generally considered to be good luck. They were thought to know where the best tin ore was to be found and could lead humans to it by the sounds of their working.

In the 1890s one old miner recounted his experiences of the knockers.

'When I was twenty years younger, I worked in Balleswidden Mine near St Just. One night I was working away for dear life, the sweat going over me like rain. I was in good heart,

A boat lies beached on the tidal banks of the River Lynher where the Wild Hunt is often seen.

because for every stroke of my tool I heard three or four clicks from the knockers, working away ahead of me. By the sound they seemed to be very near. After a few strokes the ground crumbled down loose and easy, and I found that I had broken into a vug [a hollow space in a lode of tin ore]. My eyes were dazzled at first with the glistening of the bunches of crystals of all colours which hung down from the roof and sides of the place, but when I rubbed my eyes and looked sharper into the inner end, there I spied three of the knockers. They were no bigger, either one of them, than a good sixpenny doll; yet in their faces, dress and movements, they had the look of hearty old tinners. I took the most notice of the one in the middle. He was sitting down on a stone, his jacket off and his shirt-sleeves rolled up. Between his knees he held a little anvil, no more than an inch square, yet as complete as ever you saw in a smith shop. In his left hand he held a boryer [a rod for drilling holes] about the size of a darning-needle, which he was sharpening for one of the knockers, whilst the other was waiting his turn to have the pick he held in his hand new cossened or steeled. When the knocker-smith had finished the boryer to his mind, he rested the end of the hammer on the anvil and looked toward me.

"What cheer, comrade," says he. "I couldn't think where the cold wind was coming from, and my light is blown out."

"Arrr, good morning. Is that you now," says I. "How are you? And how is all the rest of the family? I am glad to see you, and I'll fetch my candle in a wink. Your own is too small," says I, "to stand in the draught I've let into your shop. But I'll give you a pound of my candles with all my heart I will, if you've a mind to have them."

'In less than no time I turned round again with my candle in my hand. But what do you think? When I looked agin into the vug, there wasn't one of the knockers to be seen, nor their tools neither.

"Arrr then," says I. "Where are you gone to and in such a hurry? One might think you'd be glad to shake a paw with an old comrade tinner, who had been working on the same lode with you for months past."

'But all I heard was the sound of them, away somewhere in the lode ahead – tee-heeing at first then squeaking like young rabbits.'

This anonymous miner came away from his encounter well, but others were not so lucky.

A lazy miner named Barker was working in a tin mine when he heard the knockers at work. He decided that if he could steal their tools he would be able to blackmail the knockers into handing over a proportion of the ore that they had mined. He accordingly lay in wait for them one evening by a passageway that the knockers were supposed to use to get up to the surface. He planned to follow them to see where they left their tools. After a while he heard the knockers coming.

'I shall leave my tools at the bend in the stream,' said one and Barker took note.

'I shall leave mine under the bramble bush,' said a second, and Barker smiled.

'And I,' declared a third, 'will leave mine on Barker's knee.' The little man sprang up and struck Barker a mighty blow with his pick. The lazy Barker walked with a limp for the rest of his life.

At Ballowal Mine in the 1860s worked a young man named Tom Trevorrow. All the Ballowal miners were in the habit of leaving a piece of crust off their pasties for the knockers. Tom Trevorrow had none of it. He did not believe in knockers and refused to leave them anything. One evening Trevorrow was working on a narrow lode of tin ore all on his own. He stopped for a few minutes to eat a piece of fuggan, a style of heavy fruit cake popular in Cornwall. He heard a squeaky voice calling out:

'Tom Trevorrow, Tom Trevorrow,

Leave some of thy fuggan for us

Or bad luck for thee tomorrow.'

Tom thought it was his workmates playing a prank, so he shouted out 'Go to blazes you old spirits, or I'll come and knock your brains out.'

The voice called back.

'Tom Trevorrow, Tom Trevorrow,

We'll send thee bad luck tomorrow

Thou old curmudgeon to eat all thy fuggan

And not leave a diddy for the knockers.'

Next day when Tom Trevorrow reported for work he found that the passage leading to his narrow lode had caved in. All his tools were lost, as was the ore he had spent the past few days digging out. It was only the start of his bad luck and he eventually had to give up his job in the mine as none of the other miners would work with him.

A miner named Trenwith in Ransom Mine, on the other hand, did a deal with the knockers. He promised that if the knockers would show him where the best lodes were to be found, he would in return leave behind him a tenth of all the ore that he worked. The arrangement worked well, and Trenwith became a prosperous man.

John Thomas of St Just had even more to thank the knockers for, crediting the fact that he survived an accident to the intervention of the little men. His story was told by the local vicar, the Revd R.J. Noall, in a letter he wrote on 22 January 1784:

'John Thomas of this parish is aged about 62 years. He has been a notorious drunkard the greatest part of his life. Two Sundays past at about 7 o'clock in the evening he left Sancreed in order to go to his home in St Just. As it was dark and he was drunk he missed his way and fell into a pit about five fathoms deep. On his being missed, his friends made a diligent search for him, but to no purpose. The next sabbath as one of his neighbours was going to tend his sheep, he saw at some distance a little man sitting on the bank which had been thrown up in digging the pit. On going nearer he saw the little man go around to the other side of the bank. He heard a voice from the pit and thought it was some smugglers gone to hide their liquors. But as he could hear only one voice he thought it must be John Thomas and on calling found that he was not mistaken. On this he went to get help and they soon got him out of the pit. There had been a small current of water in the pit of which he drank freely. This was the means of keeping him alive. As I am not fond of crediting stories of this kind on common report, I resolved to get the account from his own mouth.'

CHAPTER 4

MYSTERIOUS TREASURES

Nobody seriously doubts that great treasures lie hidden beneath the soil of Cornwall. They have, after all, been found often enough. The vast majority of these treasures are ancient coins. While their quantity and value may vary greatly, they do tend to have a common origin.

In past centuries, when there were no such things as bank accounts, credit facilities or even bank notes, most people kept their wealth in the form of coins. Before around 1920 these coins were made of bronze, silver and gold and contained the precise quantity of metal worth the face value of the coin. Thus a florin coin, with a face value of two shillings, contained twice as much silver as a shilling. There were occasional alterations caused by fluctuating relative values between the three metals, but generally the coinage was composed of precious metals. The design on the coin was simply a guarantee from the king that it contained the prescribed amount of metal.

While most actual wealth lay in land, buildings and goods, hard cash was the main way in which transactions were carried out, taxes paid and surplus wealth stored. Since coins were easily stolen or moved and it was hard to prove ownership, it made sense to hide them. Most homes had a hiding place that was not immediately accessible. A popular place was under the hearthstone, as this could not be reached unless the cooking fire was put out. These ruses were designed to frustrate casual burglars or passing bandits.

When serious danger threatened more secure hiding places were needed for coins. If an enemy army came by, they could be relied upon to seek out and unearth coins hidden in the more usual places. Only treasure hidden in less obvious places would survive. It was for this reason that men buried pots of coins in fields, under trees, beside bridges and the like. Such hoards usually date from times of invasion or civil war. The Wars of the Roses, the Civil War between King and Parliament, the Viking invasions and the collapse of the Roman Empire all led to violence and looting and so to the burial of treasure hoards. When the owner of the hoard was unable to retrieve it, usually due to having been killed, the treasure remained where it was hidden.

Sometimes these treasures have been turned up by accident. Ploughing has unearthed some, while building works have revealed others. The sheer scale of these treasures is often staggering. Some hoards contain thousands of coins which, even at the time they were hidden, must have been astonishingly valuable. The recovery of these treasures could deeply affect not only those who found them, but even the history of nations. In 1199 a peasant ploughed up an enormous mass of gold. The bulk of the gold was promptly seized by the landowner, Ademar of Limousin. Ademar in turn sent off a share of the gold to King Richard the Lionheart. Richard, however, found a lawyer who declared that all such treasure belonged to the king, not merely a share of it. He marched an army against Ademar of Limousin and in the petty skirmish that followed, King Richard was mortally wounded. So died the Lionheart, hero of the crusades, in an unimportant squabble over buried treasure.

If even kings and lords could come to blows over treasure, it is no wonder that more ordinary folk would treat the subject of buried treasure with awe and a great deal of interest. Back in the 1850s a cottage outside Wendron became the focus for a great deal of speculation about a buried treasure trove. The speculation arose again in the 1930s and for a third time in the 1960s. To date the truth behind this mystery has not yet been solved.

The story began in the 1850s, although the exact date is uncertain, when a tin miner was very badly injured in a blasting accident. He was carried home and a doctor called. The doctor washed the miner and bandaged his wounds, but told the man's anxious mother, his only family, that the injuries were so serious that it was highly unlikely that the man would survive. The miner's workmates took it in turns to sit up with him, administer medicines and care for him.

Left alone with a dying man and with nothing much to do for hours on end, it is hardly surprising that some of the miners got curious about the sheet hanging up on one side of the room. Those who peered behind it found themselves looking into a vertical shaft driven down through the thickness of the wall. It looked for all the world as if it were the entrance to a small tin mine. The rumour quickly spread that the dying man had found a rich lode on his own land and was mining on his own account.

The man duly died. After a suitable interval his workmates approached the grieving mother and asked permission to investigate the shaft and to split with her whatever they found. She refused very curtly and threw them out of her house. She later grew very frail and went to live with another son in Penzance.

The house was rented out to a family. Hearing of the rumoured mine shaft, they began investigating and found, next to the fireplace, a stone that could be lifted. This revealed a narrow flight of steps leading down into the ground. The man lit a candle and ventured warily down the narrow passage. After going down some 30ft or so he emerged into a small cave in which he could see some old swords and a number of wooden chests. Thinking that he had found a hidden treasure, the man stepped forward to investigate.

At that instant his candle went out and it felt as if some invisible hand gripped him around the throat. Fearing ghosts or demons, the man fled back upstairs. He slammed the stone shut behind him and swore his family to secrecy.

The years passed and in 1933 a descendant of the original miner's brother was told by his mother the family's version of events back in the 1850s. It seemed that the curious shaft was not the entrance to some private tin mine, but was found by the miner behind a plastered wall. The family story was that he had been told to tear down the plaster by a rather talkative ghost who promised him that the shaft led to an underground chamber in which there was a great treasure. The miner had cleared the shaft down to ground level and had found a flagstone set into the ground that could be lifted. Underneath that was a flight of steps. The miner had been about to investigate when he had his accident. His mother concluded that the stairs were cursed and had refused either to go down them herself or to allow anyone else to do so.

The man concluded that the two hidden staircases leading underground must in reality be one and the same. He thought that the candle had been extinguished by foul air, which could also induce a choking sensation. If he could only find the stairs and descend with a torch and breathing apparatus he might yet find the swords, chests and treasure.

Eager to solve the mystery, the man travelled to Wendron. He followed the instructions to find the mystery house and found himself at Bodilly Farm. The farmhouse was quite obviously of too recent construction to be the house in question. The man knocked on the door and told the farmer of his quest. The farmer happily pointed out to the man the site of the old house that had been demolished some years earlier. It stood adjacent to the new house.

After a good deal of digging, the men found the foundations of the old house. They followed the wall round to find the fireplace. More digging revealed a large stone and, when this was lifted, a passage was revealed. The passage was not a neat staircase, but more of a sloping corridor, roughly hewn from the ground, which was blocked by fallen stones. The two men struggled for some time, but could make little headway. They gave up.

In the 1960s the story surfaced again and another team of treasure hunters headed for the farm. They found that a large and very solid concrete cattleyard had been built over the site. Whatever lies underground near Wendron lies there still. Given the presence of the concrete, it seems unlikely that the mystery will be solved any time soon.

Another buried treasure is said to lie beneath the Med Scryfa standing stone near Penwith. This huge monolith is inscribed with words in early mediaeval Celtic that translate as Rialobran, son of Cunoval. It is said that Rialobran was a king who stood as tall as the pillar, about 9ft. He is said to be buried underneath it, together with all his treasures. In 1862 some locals decided to test the legend. They dug deep, but had found nothing by the time the stone fell over and almost killed them. The attempt was abandoned and the stone reset by local gentlemen.

The great treasure of Trencrom is guarded not by a mere stone, but by disembodied spirits called spriggins. The vast store of gold is said to belong to a giant named Trecrobben who buried it deep beneath the ramparts of the old prehistoric hillfort before he left on a journey from which he never returned. Before he went, Trecrobben set a troop of hostile entities to guard his wealth from humans.

It is said that sometime in the 19th century a local farmer decided it was worth his while to spend a few idle hours digging for the gold. At first he found nothing, but on one trip with his spade he came across a buried stone engraved with strange markings. As he was digging around the stone, the farmer noticed that a storm was brewing up, but he took no notice. When the lightning began to flash and the thunder roll, the man suddenly became aware of the fact that he was no longer alone. Climbing up to sit on the nearby rocks came a host of little men, all of them extremely ugly and glaring at him with hostility, even hatred. Wisely the farmer fled. When he returned next day there was no sign of either the inscribed stone or even of the hole he had been digging. He gave up his quest for the gold.

Another treasure lies on a beach south of Trevescan, near Land's End. Sometime around 1820 a ship was wrecked near here. Among the bodies and debris washed ashore was that of a dead Chinese lady grasping in her arms a large, ivory casket. The locals were, at first, reluctant to approach. They had never seen a Chinese person before and were worried that she might be a demon of some kind. Eventually one man did investigate. He pulled the casket from the dead woman's arms and broke it open. Out tumbled a vast store of golden coins, plus the bodies of a pair of ugly, flat-faced little dogs – presumably Pekinese. The man was instantly bitten on the arm by invisible teeth. He sprang back, only for his leg to be bitten.

The man fled. His wounds appeared to have been made by a small and vicious dog, but the man was adamant both that the dogs had been dead and that his attacker had been invisible. Despite the lure of the heap of gold coins, nobody else could be induced to go down to the cove. The dead woman, her dogs and her gold were gradually covered by the sands.

So far as can be discovered they are all still there. The size of the gold hoard has, if anything, increased over the years. It is now said that the dead woman was a daughter of the Emperor of China and that her gold was enough to fill two huge chests. If anyone can be found willing to brave the phantom dog and its invisible jaws, the truth may be discovered.

The bleak hill of Hingston Down stands just west of the Tamar River, some miles south of Launceston. The treasure that is buried here is of unknown origin, but is of massive proportions. An old rhyme goes:

Hingston Down if well wrought [dug]

Is worth London Town, dearly bought.

A similarly vast treasure of obscure origins lies buried at Cudden Point.

It is not the origin of the treasure, but its extent that is mysterious at Kennack Cove near the Lizard. This hoard is the buried treasure of Henry Avery, possibly the most successful pirate of all time. Avery was born in Cornwall, sometime around the year 1660. He went to sea as a boy and by 1691 he was captain of a ship trading slaves across the Atlantic. In 1693 he abandoned slaving and was hired by the Spanish to sail as a privateer against the

The bleak hill of Hingston Down is rumoured to hide a vast treasure.

French, the two nations then being at war. Privateers were a form of maritime mercenary who fought not for pay, but for the loot that they could capture from the enemy. Their contracts of employment, known as Letters of Marque, set out which enemies they could attack and the period of time for which they were employed. If captured, privateers were to be treated as prisoners of war, not criminals.

Avery seems to have done well. In 1695 peace came and Avery's employment ended. Rather than return to slaving, Avery turned pirate. Unlike privateers, pirates were criminals operating against the law. They attacked anyone at any time and usually acted with the utmost brutality. The punishment for piracy was death. Avery had a powerful 46-gun ship named *The Fancy*. He cruised down the west coast of Africa, capturing a number of ships.

The pirate ship of Henry Avery goes into action. He took his greatest prizes in the Indian Ocean.

The famous pirate Henry Avery from a contemporary woodcut. It is said that at least some of his fabulous treasure lies in Cornwall.

Avery spared the crews of the ships he captured. When he took an English ship, he contented himself with stealing its food stores and then let it go. He sent a letter back to England that was printed in the London newspapers. In it he declared that he had no hostile intent to the English, only against foreign ships, and signed himself 'Every Englishman's friend, Henry Avery.'

For the next few months, Avery and his crew cruised the Indian Ocean, snapping up a number of prizes. Like most pirates they put into disreputable ports to sell their loot and spend the proceeds on drink and loose women. Then, in the spring of 1695, Avery captured a ship off the mouth of the Indus River. On board was a daughter of the Moghul Emperor of India who was apparently on her way to Arabia to marry a prince. She had with her a dowry of gold and jewels of truly staggering value. Its worth in terms of modern money is thought to have been around £80 million. As captain, Avery would have got the largest share – around £8 million or so.

Avery and his men realised two things very quickly. First that they were all rich men and second that they were also marked men who could expect no mercy from the forces of law and justice. If they were to both live and enjoy their wealth they had to disappear, and fast. They decided to head for the Bahamas, where they sold their ship and some of the gold in exchange for a number of small sloops. The pirate crew then split up. A few were caught and hanged, but most changed their names and went ashore to live out their lives on their loot.

Avery himself is known to have travelled to Bideford, in Devon, where he contacted some of his relatives. He persuaded them to take some of his diamonds to Bristol to sell them. This they did. Avery gave them a share of the proceeds raised, then vanished. It was later rumoured that he had gone to Ireland to buy an estate and live out his life as a retired gentleman. The truth is unknown. Quite clearly, however, Avery had got away with it – unlike the more famous Blackbeard and Captain Kidd, both of whom ended their short piratical careers very dead at the hands of the forces of law and order.

According to Cornish legend, Avery came to live on the Lizard Peninsula, where he claimed to be a successful merchant who had decided to retire from the sea. He kept his vast treasure buried in a secret location at Kennack Cove. Whenever he ran short of money he would slip down to the cove to unearth a few more bars of gold or a diamond or two. It is said that he died young and that most of his vast treasure still lies at Kennack Cove.

It is, of course, quite unknown whether Avery actually did come to the Lizard Peninsula and, if he did, whether any of his treasure still lies at Kennack Cove. Rather more certain is the treasure that lies off Gunwalloe. In 1526 a large ship was spotted in trouble during a storm. The ship was clearly foreign and, equally clearly, was doomed. The locals gathered to watch. The ship foundered some distance off shore. There were no survivors, and only a few bodies and small pieces of wreckage were washed up on land. It was later discovered that the ship had been the *Santo Andreo*, a galleon belonging to the King of Portugal which had been heading to London with a substantial amount of gold bullion on board. No trace of the gold has ever been found, nor have modern underwater archaeologists been able to find it.

The fate of the *Santo Andreo* introduces one of the more reliable sources of treasure hunting in Cornwall: wrecking. Since the most ancient times the folk of Cornwall have assumed that they have the right to collect any pieces of flotsam and jetsam that the sea washes up on their coasts. When this was the usual debris of seafaring, not much notice was taken and indeed this activity of beachcombing goes on in most coastal areas. Wrecking is different as it involves the deliberate plundering of wrecks or of items washed ashore from a lost ship.

The activity of wrecking could take a variety of forms. At its most harmless, this meant picking up goods and items washed ashore after a ship had been accidentally wrecked. More deliberate was the entering of a wrecked ship to take away items and strip it of everything of use. More disturbing was the fact that locals often ignored the plight of survivors in their scramble to get at the valuables. Downright sinister were the occasional rumours that survivors had been murdered. There are very few examples of proven murder, if for no other reason than there was no real need for it. Even if survivors of a wreck decided to complain to the forces of law and order, it was highly unlikely that they would be able to identify those who had been engaged in plundering.

Worst of all was the alleged activity of deliberately leading ships astray so that they would be wrecked. It was said that on stormy nights lanterns would be lit in a cove to simulate the appearance of a safe harbour. Ships would approach, and their crews not realise the trick until it was too late and the ship was doomed. Then the wreckers would move in to murder the crew and steal what they could. A 17th-century man named Killigrew was alleged to have gained wealth in this way, but the case was never proven. Nor was any other case of deliberate wrecking, but the rumours continued.

In fact, wrecking was, for most of recorded history, an occasional practice that brought little real money to the Cornish. It was not until the 1600s that plundering wrecked ships grew as an activity. The massive increase in international trade, particularly to Asia and the Americas, that took place around this time meant that large numbers of ships captained by men unfamiliar with Cornwall's coasts were passing on their way to Bristol or up the Channel to London, Antwerp and other ports. When bad weather struck these ships were vulnerable to being driven onto rocks, shoals or headlands with which their crews were unfamiliar. By the later 18th century improved charts and navigational skills meant that fewer ships were wrecked, though enough still came ashore to tempt the wreckers.

An early example of wrecking is recorded in a letter sent by Richard Drinkwater of Truro to Sir Richard Edgcumbe on 6 February 1672. After recounting how he was riding toward Mevagissey the previous day, Drinkwater said that he came upon a crowd of local farm workers heading for Chappel Head and decided to follow them. 'Att length I espyed a shipps hull there and only ye maine maste up. I made all the speed downe I could possible, and found it to bee a vessel of 400 tons, ye water ebbing away, ye country comes in and cut and hew down sayles and mastes and ankers and cables, and carry them away.'

The fact that Cornish wreckers were not entirely heartless is shown by the case of the German ship *Vigilantia*, which was wrecked at Perranuthnoe in November 1738. The local fishermen pulled the mate and five men from the sea on their first trip out to the wreck, though the captain and three others were pulled out dead from drowning. Only then did the fishermen go back to loot the ship. Once everything of any worth had been removed, they went back and spent a couple of days dismantling the ship itself. By the time Charles Vyvyan of the Penzance Customs arrived to take charge there was nothing left of the ship at all. The German survivors were, however, safe and sound, well fed and reclothed.

A real wrecking mystery occurred at Porthleven in January 1768. A ship of about 500 tons was driven ashore during a gale. The ship was quite intact, so the locals swarmed aboard. They found not a single living thing on board, neither man nor beast. Nor were there any documents to show where the ship was from, who owned it or what it was called. The only clue was a wooden board hung in the captain's cabin that was written in Dutch. It translated as:

'When we are at sea my cabin is here
In a jiffy I can reach the deck
If something happens I can hear it right away
Which often disturbs my rest.'

What the ship was and why it had been abandoned remain a mystery to this day.

The legal position of wrecking was always slightly obscure. Strictly speaking goods washed ashore from an unknown source were the property of the owner of the land where they came to rest. Property that came from an identifiable source – such as a wreck – remained the property of the original owner. However, wreckers could claim rights of salvage by rescuing the goods from the waves. In this case they could claim a reward from the owner if he turned up and asked for the return of his goods. If the owner did not demand its return within a rather vaguely defined period of time, the salvager could keep the item. In practice this meant that the wreckers kept what they could take.

From about 1790 the situation began to change. The threat of invasion from Napoleonic France meant that large numbers of troops were stationed around the Cornish coast. These men were available to the local magistrates and were often called out to a wreck. Once the soldiers were about the local wreckers turned to respectable salvage. The system was that they gathered up items of value from the wreck, then handed them over to the military officer who took a note of who had recovered what. When the shipowner was traced he was asked to pay for the return of the items. If he did, the reward was shared out among the salvagers, if not the goods were auctioned off and the proceeds divided.

By 1800 the insurance men of Lloyds in London had moved in to accompany the military. They took to patrolling the coast in rough weather, and often had the soldiers on the spot before the weather had calmed enough to allow wreckers to plunder the ship. In the 1830s the prosecution of men who had taken goods from wrecks and then not handed them over to insurance agents began. One of the first was Thomas Ellis of St Just, who was sentenced to six months in prison for taking a barrel of wine from a French wreck. The local newspaper thought the sentence rather on the harsh side since Ellis had helped to rescue the crew before going back for the wine.

The case of Thomas Ellis was, at the time, held up to be the end of wrecking. Of course, it was not. In 1878 a Spanish steamer named the *Ana* came ashore at Morvah. The crew and passengers were rescued by fishermen, who then returned to strip the ship. So much was got out that the goods were traded across Cornwall.

More recently, in January 2007, the cargo ship *Napoli* ran ashore off Branscombe. The ship was holed and hundreds of containers of goods fell into the sea to be washed ashore, at first on Branscombe Beach but later as far east as Hampshire. A huge variety of items from bottles of shampoo to BMW motorbikes came ashore. Soon the beach was swarming with people keen to pick up what they could. Within 24 hours the police had arrived and, as in days of old, were collecting the goods and logging who had found what. Once it became clear, however, that rewards were unlikely to be offered the public lost interest in helping. A special clean-up team had to be formed to collect the debris. Even so, smaller items continued to be washed up for weeks, to the delight of the locals.

Such treasures that still lie in Cornwall are probably pots of coins buried in troubled times long gone. Though when a new treasure will be washed up from a wreck nobody knows.

CHAPTER 5

MYSTERIOUS ARTHUR

The mighty King Arthur is a figure familiar to many, be it from television shows, Hollywood movies or story books. These show Arthur as a powerful mediaeval king surrounded by a band of heroic knights intent on doing chivalrous deeds of various kinds, usually for the benefit of winsomely beautiful ladies. This King Arthur is brought low by the treachery of his half-sister Morgana and her son Mordred. It is a dramatic and heroic epic of vast scope and proportions.

These stories are all based on mediaeval poems and stories that pictured Arthur as being the epitome of the code of chivalry that was then fashionable among the warrior elite of Europe. He was said to rule over Britain from his court at Camelot and was supported by the Knights of the Round Table. It was all a fantasy conjured up by poets and writers seeking to create an imaginary backdrop against which to set their romances and songs. This Arthur was said to have lived at some point in the distant past, ruling over a lost paradise of knightly virtues. It is largely because these stories and the Arthur figure in them were so patently false that some scholars have sought to prove that Arthur himself never existed.

However, the mediaeval romancers chose Arthur's court in which to set their stories because he was already widely famous as a powerful and noble ruler from days gone by. Direct evidence as to who Arthur had been and when he had lived was even then scarce, and now is even rarer, but it seems clear that if he lived at all it must have been in the poorly recorded Dark Ages after the fall of the Roman Empire.

The good people of Cornwall have their own distinctive take on the mystery of King Arthur. Nobody found this out more quickly, or more dramatically, than nine French monks who came to Cornwall in the year 1113. The monks were on a fundraising mission for the cathedral at Tours. They were carrying a collection of holy relics which they were charging people to see and touch. On their journeys through the south west of England they had several times heard stories about Arthur and his exploits. When they arrived in Bodmin, the French monks exposed their relics in the parish church. Among those who came to see them was a local man with a crippled arm who was hoping to be cured. As the crippled man approached the subject of Arthur came up. The man told the monks that Arthur was still alive. The monks laughed at him and assured him that Arthur was dead. The other locals took the side of the cripple and the discussion soon became a dispute that escalated into a fistfight. The local lord sent in his men to restore order, which they did with difficulty. The monks found it wise to move on.

It is clear from this incident both that the Bodmin locals felt strongly about Arthur and that they believed that he was still alive. What is not so often noticed is that the French monks were equally convinced that Arthur was a real person, only differing in their view that he was a ruler who had died many years previously. The incident is important as it predates the more elaborate mediaeval romances and so gives a clue about the Arthur that the romancers reworked for their own purposes.

By far the most famous Arthurian place in Cornwall is Tintagel, on the north coast, which is said to have been his birthplace. There is a dramatic castle perched 250ft above the sea on a small promontory linked to the mainland by the narrowest of rocky paths. The nearby village has long made a good living out of its Arthurian links with teashops, souvenir shops and other emporia named after Arthur, Camelot or other elements of the Arthurian legend.

The link to Arthur first appears in the 1140s in the writings of Geoffrey of Monmouth, the first of the mediaeval writers to devote much time to Arthur. According to Geoffrey, Uther, King of Britain, fell in love with Ygraine, the wife of Duke Gorlois of Cornwall. Gorlois would not give up his wife so war followed. Ygraine was placed in Tintagel Castle for safety while the battles raged. Uther consulted the wizard Merlin, who magically transformed him so that he looked exactly like Gorlois. Using this disguise, Uther was admitted to Tintagel, where he spent the night with Ygraine. Arthur was the product of this illicit night. When Gorlois was killed in battle, the war ended. Ygraine married Uther to become Queen of Britain.

Arthur, meanwhile, had been handed over to Merlin as the price Uther had agreed to pay for the magic. Merlin knew that Uther's reign was about to decline into incompetence and unrest, so he sent Arthur off to live with the good knight Sir Kay where he would be safe until he was a grown man and was ready to become king in his turn.

The ruins to be seen at Tintagel today date back to 1141 when Reginald, Earl of Cornwall, built a fortress here. The castle was renovated and altered many times over the years, so the standing walls are mostly of 13th-century date. Interestingly, archaeologists have found traces of habitations dating back to the time of Arthur. The foundations of stone and timber buildings have been found, while fragments of costly pottery imported from the Mediterranean show that whoever lived here was rich and probably powerful. It may well have been a fortress inhabited by the ruler of Cornwall.

In the 1990s a fresh archaeological excavation turned up a tantalising piece of evidence that hit the nation's headlines. As well as additional evidence of a rich household standing here in the late fifth and early sixth centuries, the dig turned up a broken slab of stone engraved in Latin. The inscription was broken, but seemed to translate as 'Paternus descendant of Coll and Artognous descendant of Coll had this made.' The Press pounced, encouraged by the excavators, and made much of the similarity between 'Arthur' and 'Artognous'. Unfortunately, there does not seem to be a meaningful historic link.

At the base of the rock on which Tintagel Castle stands is a cave that runs right through the promontory. This is known today as Merlin's Cave. It is a dramatic place, especially

The inner ramparts of Castle-an-Dinas, which has two different links to the great King Arthur.

when the tide surges through it, but its links to the master wizard seem tenuous. Some miles south of Tintagel stand the dramatic ramparts of the pre-Roman hillfort of Castle-an-Dinas. The site has not been properly excavated, and it is unclear whether or not it was reoccupied in post-Roman times like several of these ancient strongholds. It has two links with Arthur.

The first is to be found in a mediaeval romance which names Castle Dinas as the site of the battle in which Duke Gorlois was killed on the same night as Arthur was conceived at Tintagel. The second is a local legend that the hillfort was once King Arthur's hunting lodge. A book written in 1400, but preserving oral traditions of early but uncertain date, says that Arthur had a hilltop castle in this area of Cornwall that was destroyed by Mordred's men after the final battle between uncle and nephew.

Whatever the truth, Castle-an-Dinas is a magnificent palace to visit. The three rings of ramparts are largely intact, while the summit offers magnificent views across the Vale of Mawgan and surrounding hills.

Another version of the death of Gorlois places it in the churchyard of St Dennis. This is an earlier reference than that to Castle-an-Dinas and places the death as occurring during a battle to capture the fortress of 'Dimilioc'. There is no such place today, but the Domesday Book of 1086 records that the hill on which the church stands is called 'Dimilihoc', which

The ancient stone cross in the churchyard of St Dennis. This may, possibly, be old enough to have stood here in the days when King Arthur was a visitor.

is almost identical. It is certainly possible. The circular churchyard wall follows the route of a defensive ditch and bank that dates back to Arthurian times.

Just inside the gate to the churchyard stands a stone cross that has been dated to the fifth century. The fact that this whole area is used as a churchyard has made archaeological excavation impossible, but the evidence does point to this site being a fortified base, perhaps with a small monastery, at the time that Gorlois is supposed to have ruled Cornwall.

The church that occupies the site today is well worth a visit. The oldest stone church here was begun in about 1080, but entirely replaced in the 14th century. That church was in turn replaced in 1847 – only the tower was left standing. The church of 1847 was in turn burned down in 1985, but it has been rebuilt. The result is a remarkable blend of styles and designs.

Most versions of the Arthurian legend cycle take Arthur out of Cornwall once he had been born and given to Merlin. He does not return until near the end of his life. There are, however, a few local links to him. Most of these are brief and add little to our knowledge of Arthur either in history or legend. They do, however, prove that Arthur was a popular figure in Cornwall. Arthur is said to have fought an evil giant who lived on St Michael's Mount. Arthur was victorious and threw the giant's body into Mount's Bay, where its bones still lie. He is said to have killed other giants at Pendeen.

Among the oldest written references to Arthur is a manuscript which says he came from Kelliwic. While this place has not been identified with any real certainty, the old hillfort above Killibury is a strong contender. Arthur is said to have had a mighty palace at Trereen Dinas, and another on the hills above St Breward. This later site has prehistoric stone structures that are named Arthur's Hall and Arthur's Trough. Another ancient stone, this

King Arthur is said to have fought an evil giant who lived on St Michael's Mount.

time lying flat on the ground high on Bodmin Moor, is called Arthur's Bed. A larger stone near St Columb Major has four indentations carved into it that are supposed to have been left by the hooves of Arthur's war horse.

At Zennor, Arthur is said to have stopped to eat lunch with four Cornish kings during a campaign to rid the area of an invading army of red-headed Danes. The same story is told of the prehistoric stone monument of Table Men at Mayon. This legend does at least give a vague date for Arthur. If he was involved in fighting off Viking invaders of Cornwall he must have lived around 850. Unfortunately our written records for that date are fairly complete and reliable. We know that there was no King Arthur at that time, and neither were there any Cornish kings, as by that date the area had become part of the English kingdom of Wessex.

The village of Gerrans is linked to Arthur only indirectly. It is said to be the burial place of Gerient, one of the leading Knights of the Round Table. His funeral barge is said to have brought his body here from the place where he died, rowed by oarsmen using silver oars. This Gereint provides a tenuous link between Arthur and real history. He was killed fighting against an invading force of Saxons at Portchester in Hampshire in or about the year 501. A poem written only a few years later says that he was fighting alongside men of Arthur's army.

Another Arthurian figure, Cadwy, is said to be buried in the Cadon Barrow near Camelford. Cadwy was a king of Cornwall, though his dates are entirely uncertain. Later legend made him the son of Gorlois and Ygraine and so Arthur's elder half-brother. He is said to have been the last ruler in Britain to acknowledge that Arthur was the rightful King of Britain. Having finally admitted this, Cadwy remained utterly loyal and died alongside Arthur in the final battle against the treacherous Mordred.

The site of that final, fatal battle is given in some of the earliest manuscripts as being at Camlann. Unfortunately no place of that name now exists. Either the name has changed over the years, or the place lay in that part of Britain later conquered by the English and so has a quite different name. The name Camlann is derived from early Welsh words meaning 'crooked banks', which would seem to indicate that it was fought on the banks of a winding river.

Geoffrey of Monmouth claimed to have found in an 'ancient book' the fact that the winding river in question was the Camel, in Cornwall. A mass grave was found near the river in Tudor times. These two links served to fix the site of the battle at Slaughterbridge, at least so far as local legend was concerned. The more romantic later legends make this battle the culminating conflict in a civil war between the by now elderly Arthur and his treacherous nephew Mordred.

The supporters of both leaders persuaded the men to meet for a parley to see if a peaceful solution could be found to the kingdom's problems. The two armies were drawn up facing each other and it was decided that Arthur and Mordred would step forward, accompanied by only a few men, to talk. To guard against treachery, no man was allowed to draw any weapon at all. Just as the talking began, however, an adder slid out of the grass and made to strike one of Arthur's men. Without thinking, the man drew a sword to kill the snake. This was seen by Mordred's men, who suspected treachery and attacked. Both Arthur and Mordred were killed in the fighting, though one version has it that Arthur was carried off to the magical otherworldly kingdom of Avalon to rest and recuperate until such time as his people needed him again.

A short distance upstream of Slaughterbridge there is an ancient stone tomb that, according to local legend recorded as early as the 1600s, is that of King Arthur. Certainly the letters ATRY were seen carved into it. Unfortunately the stone has since been excavated and modern techniques have allowed the inscription to be read in its entirety. It is of Dark Age date, but it translates as 'The monument of Latinus. Here he lies, the son of Magarus'.

Some distance away, high on Bodmin Moor, lies Dozmary Pool. This small lake can be a bleak, windswept place. It is said to be the place where Sir Bedivere threw Arthur's sword Excalibur to the Lady of the Lake after the Battle of Camlann. The atmospheric tarn certainly feels like the sort of place where this might have happened, but it is probably not.

Slaughterbridge as it was in the 1890s before the old bridge was taken down and replaced with one better suited for motor traffic. King Arthur is said to have received his death wound here.

Dozmary Pool stands high on Bodmin Moor. It is said to be the place where Sir Bedivere threw Arthur's sword Excalibur to the Lady of the Lake.

The link between Arthur, Excalibur and the Lady of the Lake did not emerge until the mediaeval romances were written, and Sir Bedivere came into the story even later. In any case it is miles from Slaughterbridge, so Sir Bedivere stood little chance of getting there and back in the time available. The same story is claimed for Loe Pool, a tidal bay off Mount's Bay.

It is difficult to be certain about exactly what lies behind all these stories and legends. Vast numbers of books have been written about Arthur over the years, and yet no firm conclusion has been reached. There are so many layers of legend and meaning overlaid on each other that it is almost impossible to be certain of anything. Put simply, however, there are two basic schools of thought.

The first holds that there was never a historic person called Arthur at all. It is pointed out that his exploits of killing giants, leaving hoofprints in solid stone and the like are more usual among gods than among real men. It has been suggested that he was a pagan deity who survived into Christian times as a mythical hero, later to be misinterpreted by mediaeval romancers. It is certainly true that some of the figures in the Arthurian cycle are of pagan origin. For instance, the figure of Sir Kay is derived from the old god Cei. Other figures that do have some historic base are scattered over three centuries of history, so it would seem that these real men have been linked to a mythical figure to enhance their reputations. The supporters of this idea suggest that all apparent documentary evidence for Arthur's existence was created by later chroniclers inserting the name of a famous person to enliven otherwise dull accounts of long-ago events.

It has been suggested that Arthur's name was originally Artor, meaning the ploughman. This would have made him an agricultural divinity, which might account for his popularity with farming folk. There is, however, no archaeological nor documentary evidence for a god named Artor, nor for one who had the plough as his symbol.

The second school of thought sees Arthur as having been a real man whose exploits were later enhanced and embellished as legend took over. This scenario takes the written sources more seriously, suggesting that they are genuine early accounts copied by later writers. This view sees Arthur as a ruler and war leader who led the Romano-Britons against the barbarians as the Roman Empire collapsed. The Battle of Badon Hill is known to have taken place around the year 500 and was probably fought somewhere between the lower Severn and upper Thames. The manuscript naming Arthur as the British commander was written about the year 900, but is almost certainly a copy of a document written within living memory of the battle. Other early written sources for Arthur are all internally consistent and place him between the years 480 and 540, making him a commander of British armies against the invading English.

Given the geopolitical face of Britain at the time, it is unlikely that Arthur came from Cornwall. At the time Cornwall – along with Devon and most of Somerset and Dorset –

formed part of the kingdom of Dumnonia. The later kings of Dumnonia did not claim any direct link to Arthur as they surely would have done had he come from their lands or been an ancestor. He is more likely to have originated in one of the rich, lowland areas of Britain that were later to become England. He was remembered so clearly in Cornwall, as he was in Wales, because it was there that the descendants of the people he led survived. The English enemy did not remember him at all. The memory of Arthur was retained only in those parts of southern Britain that the English did not conquer.

It is most likely that he was a real man, but that the accretions of legend and storytelling have enhanced his exploits to such an extent that they have assumed mythical qualities. Certainly no man can have done a fraction of what Arthur is supposed to have achieved. The way in which legend can twist and confuse history is shown very clearly in Cornwall in relation to an Arthurian figure of great importance, the wizard Merlin. As already mentioned, there is a Merlin's Cave at Tintagel, but he is remembered elsewhere in Cornwall.

At Mousehole there is Merlin's Rock jutting out from the cliff to the south of the harbour wall. There the wizard is said to have uttered a prophecy that an invader who landed on his rock would achieve success over the Cornish. This was later formalised as the lines:

'There shall land on the stone of Merlin

Those who shall burn Paul, Penzance and Newlyn.'

Merlin's Rock, off Mousehole, is linked to a prophecy allegedly made by King Arthur's court magician.

The rhyme is first recorded in 1596, the year after a force of Spanish soldiers landed on Merlin's Rock, going on to burn St Paul's Church in Mousehole as well as Penzance and Newlyn.

Merlin is said to have uttered another prophecy at St Levan. Pointing to the narrow crack in a boulder there he is supposed to have said:

'When with panniers astride
A packhorse can ride
Through St Levan's stone
The world will be done.'

Merlin made a similarly gloomy prediction about the Lanyon Quoit that stands on the moorland Madron. This is the ruin of a prehistoric tomb that takes the form of a heavy rock set horizontally on top of three others. It therefore resembles a giant table. Arthur and his knights are said to have used the Lanyon Quoit as a table for lunch on their way to fight the Battle of Camlann. Merlin ate in silence and appeared most depressed. When Arthur asked Merlin why he was so upset, Merlin replied that he had seen in a vision that they would never dine together again until they returned to the Lanyon Quoit to eat a meal on the eve of Doomsday.

What makes these stories about Merlin interesting is that they all originated long after the mediaeval romances linked Merlin to Arthur. It seems that the local people adopted the master wizard only after he had become tied to their existing hero. Merlin, in fact, was a very different person who lived at a different time from Arthur.

He was born in Wales as Myrddin Wyllt around 540. He was a famous bard and holy man who served King Gwenddoleu of Gwynedd. In 573 he was present at the Battle of Arfderydd, where the men of Gwenddoleu were defeated and then massacred by the forces of King Riderch of Strathclyde. Myrddin went mad and fled into the forests, where he lived as a wild man. It was there that he is said to have gained the gift of prophecy. A huge number of legends are told of him thereafter, but most of the early tales are connected to Wales and Cumbria.

Myrddin became Merlin in the hands of the mediaeval romancers. They changed his name, as Myrddin was close to a French word of unpleasant connotations and brought him into the Arthurian cycle to give him a strong legendary background. Only then did he make his way into Cornish stories. But Arthur and Merlin are not the only ancient figures to enter into Cornish mysteries.

CHAPTER 6

MYSTERIOUS HISTORY

The past is a living thing in Cornwall. Each village hands on its stories about the past and about local characters. Some of these tales can be traced through the written record to real people and real events. But a few rely entirely on local hearsay handed down from generation to generation – what ethnologists call 'folk memory'. Inevitably the facts can sometimes get jumbled up, different stories get merged together and bits forgotten. But for a good deal of this mysterious history there does seem to have been some element of fact that started the stories off in the first place.

Take, for instance, the legend of the Druid's Cup of Rillaton. According to this tale a druid used to live by the Cheesewring, a megalithic standing stone high on Bodmin Moor. He was in the habit of sitting in a stone formation dubbed the Druid's Chair, in order to pass judgement on those who came to him to consult his learning and wisdom. He also had a fabulous golden cup, which had the magical property that it could never be drunk dry. Into this the druid would put a magical potion that restored and revived anyone who drank it. Travellers and hunters alike made a point of stopping at the Druid's Chair to take refreshment.

One fateful day a party of hunters from Trewortha were having a terrible day up on Bodmin Moor, not having caught a thing by the time dusk began to close in. Tired and dispirited, they decided to head for the Cheesewring to sup from the druid's cup. One of the hunters declared that he was so thirsty that he would drain the cup dry. His companions, who knew better, jeered at him.

When the hunting party approached the druid, he offered them his cup and each man drank his fill before passing it on. When the man who had boasted he would drain it got hold of the cup, he tipped it back and gulped down the potion in vast quantities. No matter how much he drank, the cup was always about half full when he took it from his lips. Finally, bloated beyond comfort, the man lost his temper. He hurled the contents of the golden cup into the face of the druid, then rode off, brandishing the cup over his head and shouting back insults.

The rider did not get far. His horse bolted, then threw him as it stumbled over rocks. The man fell awkwardly, breaking his neck and being killed instantly. The hunting party found him dead and cold next morning. They retrieved the cup and carried it back to the Cheesewring, but the druid had gone and was never seen again. Nobody wanted to keep the cup, so it was buried with the thief beneath a pile of stones where the horse had thrown him. That mound of rocks was covered with turf and so became Rillaton Barrow.

In 1818 a group of antiquarians, as the amateur archaeologists of the time were called, decided to open Rillaton Barrow to see what it contained. They found that it was a typical chambered burial mound of the Bronze Age. Inside was the body of a man who had been buried with spear, shield and a gold cup. This beautiful little beaker was presented to the Prince Regent and remained in the possession of the Royal Family until the 1920s when King George V presented it to the British Museum, where it remains to this day.

The story of the huntsman buried with a golden cup would seem to have been borne out by the discovery of the gold cup inside the barrow. Presumably the dead man was a local lord or warrior who had been buried with his possessions some 3,000 years ago. Although his existence would seem to have been remembered across all these generations, the rest of the story, with its magical potions and druids, cannot be part of the original account.

Not only is the fully developed story more akin to a tale about fairies than real life, but the elements don't fit together. The druids did not appear in Britain until some 750 years after the dead man and his cup were buried in the Rillaton Barrow. There is no evidence, apart from this tale, that any druid ever sat on the Druid's Chair, nor that one had anything to do with the Cheesewring. In fact the story has some marked similarities to tales about the theft of magical items from their owners that are told elsewhere, except that those stories usually feature fairies, not druids. It seems likely that the original story featured a fairy, but that this was transformed into a druid when the story was linked to the Cheesewring.

It is unfortunate that the earliest written record of this legend dates back to a few years after the barrow was excavated. There must therefore be the suspicion that the legend was invented to explain the cup. This, however, cannot be proved. Certainly the man who collected the story, the Revd Sabine Baring-Gould, was convinced that the story had been current before the excavation. He was there and we are not, so there seems no real reason to disbelieve him.

Down the estuary from Padstow is a sacred spring dedicated to St George. The flow of water never fails, no matter how dry the summer, and the waters have long been rumoured to have curative powers. They are also, if local legend is to be believed, touched by the divine.

One day, many centuries ago, a ship passing off shore came into the mouth of the Camel. A group of men came ashore looking for water. One of the men touched the ground and a spring of sweet, pure water burst forth. The sailors filled their kegs, then went back to sea and sailed away. That man, the story says, was Jesus Christ.

It is a simple tale, almost stark. By itself it is almost nonsensical, but it forms part of a wider cycle of stories about a visit by Jesus Christ to the south west of Britain. Most of these stories relate to sites in Devon or Somerset, the story about Padstow being the only one with a direct link to Cornwall. Taken together the stories do make some sort of sense, though that does not mean that they are true.

The key figure in the stories is Joseph of Arimathea. In the Bible, Joseph of Arimathea makes only a fairly brief appearance in the Gospels, though all four do agree on his actions and background. According to the Gospels, Joseph of Arimathea was a wealthy man and a member of the Sanhedrin, the supreme religious council of the Jews at the time. He is described as being a secret follower of Jesus during the time when Jesus was preaching in Jerusalem. After the crucifixion, Joseph went to see Pontius Pilate and asked permission to take the body of Jesus away for burial. This was usually a duty of the next of kin, though the Gospels say that Joseph acted as he did because he was worried that some of the Jews might desecrate the body. Working with a man named Nicodemus who was a Pharisee, or learned theologian, Joseph washed the body, treated it with myrrh and aloes and then buried it in a new tomb that he had acquired.

Joseph of Arimathea then vanishes from the Gospels, but not from later traditions. These made Joseph into an uncle of the Virgin Mary, the mother of Jesus. This might explain his interest in the body. He is also said to have been a rich merchant, and it is this that is usually taken as the base for the stories of Christ's visit to Britain.

One of the most profitable trades for merchants operating out of the Middle East at the time – if they were willing to take the risks involved – was the tin trade. Ships sailed west across the Mediterranean, then out of the Straits of Gibraltar before turning north to sail up the Spanish coast and across the Bay of Biscay to reach Cornwall and its rich tin mines. If Joseph of Arimathea was a rich tin merchant he would have sailed this route many times.

If Joseph of Arimathea was the great-uncle of Jesus Christ, it would have been more than likely that the boy's poor parents might have sent him off to work as an apprentice for his rich relative for a while. The Gospels are, indeed, silent about what Jesus did between the ages of about 13 and 30. Perhaps he was away from home working for his rich uncle Joseph.

If Jesus was so employed, he would have been sent off on various missions to keep an eye on the family business, and one such mission may well have been to take part in a voyage to the tin mines. This would explain why several places in the south-west of Britain have legends and folktales about a visit from Jesus Christ. Strikingly these stories are found only in the one area of Britain that he might conceivably have visited.

Be that as it may, the links between the south-west and Christ do not end there. It is said that after Christ's resurrection and ascension, Joseph of Arimathea got into trouble with the Roman authorities. He had to flee, so he sold all his belongings for cash. Joseph then gathered together a band of early Christian converts and set sail to seek safety. He had to get beyond the reach of Rome, so he naturally headed for the tin mining areas where he had contacts and which at this time were not part of the Roman Empire.

He seems to have spent some years travelling about Cornwall and Devon. Then, in the year 63AD, he was climbing a hill in Somerset when he struck his staff into the ground and turned to his Christian companions declaring 'We are weary all.' The staff instantly took root and began to grow into a tree. Joseph and his followers took this to be a divine sign that their wanderings were over. They built a small church and founded Britain's first permanent

Christian community at the foot of the hill. That place is now Glastonbury and the hill is called Wirral Hill.

It is difficult to know what to make of these stories. They are persistent, early and not totally beyond the bounds of possibility. It must be accepted, however, that when the monk William of Malmesbury was writing a history of Glastonbury in 1135 he found that the earliest references to a Christian church on the site dated back to only 180, and even that reference was rather obscure. The monks of Glastonbury objected to William's version and claimed he had not looked at their most ancient texts. The documents that William consulted were lost in the Reformation, as were those referred to by the Glastonbury monks – if they ever actually existed.

The best that can be said with any certainty is that Christianity took hold very early in the south west. It was a major religion here long before the fall of the Roman Empire. Certainly the holy men in the area were in a position to know whether or not Joseph of Arimathea or even Jesus Christ himself had ever visited Cornwall. They seem to have believed that Joseph had and that Christ might have done. Today, we have no way of knowing.

One of the more persistent but shadowy figures of Cornish legend is King Gerennius. The name is a latinised version of the Celtic name Gereint, which is also sometimes rendered as Gerontius. This king is said to have lived sometime after the fall of the Roman Empire but before the complete ascendancy of the English. His wealth was proverbial, as was his wisdom and learning. He is usually said to be buried beneath the huge barrow on Nare Head that overlooks Gerrans Bay, probably named after the king.

According to legend King Gerennius lived at a place called Dingerein, which translates from early Celtic to mean 'Gereint's Fortress'. This is traditionally said to be Veryan Castle, an oval earthwork near Gwendra. The king was a follower of St Teilo, an equally famous Cornish saint of this murky period. The two performed many wonderful deeds. When King Gerennius died it was St Teilo who performed the burial rites.

Historians have long argued about whether this fabulous king ever actually lived. The problem is that the history of the Cornish royal dynasty was not preserved and we have only references to them preserved in other works. We know that the dynasty came originally from the upper Severn valley, most likely from somewhere near Shrewsbury. As the leader of a military force Docco of the Cornovii was moved to the south west by order of the post-Roman government of Britain in about the year 420. His task was to drive off Irish raiders who were pillaging the area. He did this with great success and his descendants continued to rule the area, under the authority of the central government of Britain.

When the last vestiges of post-Roman British unity died with King Arthur in about 540, the Cornovii became independent rulers of a kingdom called Dumnonia after the largest Celtic tribe of the area. The precise borders of Dumnonia are uncertain. It certainly included what are now Devon and Cornwall. It also included parts of what is now Dorset, perhaps all of that area. Somerset at least as far north as Glastonbury was also part of Dumnonia. Over the centuries that followed the invading English gradually pushed the Celtic rulers back until by around 750 all that was left to them were the lands west of the Tamar. That rump of a kingdom was by this date known as Cornwall, taking its name from the ruling family, the Cornovii.

Cornwall eventually lost its independence soon after the year 800. It is not certain whether the English kingdom of Wessex conquered Cornwall or if the two came together to face the then growing menace of the Vikings. Certainly the Earls of Cornwall seem to have retained some form of local rule under the Wessex kings, but details are vague.

King Gerennius must belong to the period between 550 and 800 when the kings of Cornwall were independent. The link to St Teilo would put him in around the year 640, perhaps a bit earlier. Dumnonia was certainly a large and powerful kingdom at this time, so later generations may have remembered a king ruling at this time as being both rich and wise, as Gerennius features in legend.

Historians have tried to identify this Gerennius in the written record, but without much success. One Gereint of the Cornovii, who died in around 480, is too early. So is another Gereint of uncertain lineage who was killed fighting the English in 508 in what is now Hampshire. A Gerontius, a contemporary of Arthur, might be the first Dumnonian to be independent and so might have been remembered. Other men named Gereint or Gerontius crop up in the historical record at periods, but none of them seems closely linked to Dumnonia or to the Cornovii.

Whoever he was in reality, King Gerennius has suffered in legend compared to another mysterious ruler of Cornwall, King Mark. This King Mark seems to have lived around the year 570 and to have had his main residence at Castle Dore, near St Sampson. He had a son named Drustan who died before he inherited the throne. The dates of Mark's reign cannot be established for certain, but French records show that a nobleman named Idwal fled to King Childebert in 557 seeking protection from King Mark. It is recorded that this Mark married four times, mostly for political reasons. From the asides made by monkish scribes it seems that at least one of those marriages was bigamous, though neither Mark nor his brides seem to have been bothered.

The reason why King Mark became so famous is that long after his death he and his son Drustan became the subject of a series of romantic poems and tales invented by minstrels and troubadours. These stories called Drustan, Tristan and made him Mark's nephew instead of his son. The stories pushed Mark's rule back about 60 years so that it coincided with the rule of King Arthur. That allowed them to make Tristan one of the Knights of the Round Table.

The legends of Mark and Tristan are too long and involved to retell in great detail. In essence, the legends made the much-married Mark a lecherous old tyrant. He was said to lust after beautiful young noblewomen and used his wealth and power to force their reluctant fathers to hand them over as brides. But as soon as Mark tired of a wife she would meet with a fatal accident and so clear the way for the next young bride.

At some point in this murderous marriage career, Mark fell for Iseult, daughter of an Irish nobleman. Young Tristan was sent to collect the new bride. Before he left Cornwall he was given a magical love potion that he was to give to Iseult just before she met Mark. This would cause her to fall in love with the lustful old man and so go happily to her doom. Of course (such is the way of mediaeval romances) the potion was mistakenly taken by Tristan and Iseult while on the ship carrying them from Ireland to Cornwall. The two fell passionately in love. The results of this were long, complex and predictably tragic for all concerned.

The story seems to have reached more or less its final form in Wales around the year 1000. It grew to be enormously popular, not only in Britain but also in France, Spain, Italy and Germany. The legend was retold in many versions and languages, some of which remain in print to this day. No doubt it was this huge popularity that ensured that Mark and Tristan were remembered when so many other men of that era were forgotten.

Castle Dore is named in many versions as the home of King Mark, though a few place it at nearby Lantyan Manor. Castle Dore stands in the parish of Lantyan, so that when early writers put down the location of the palace as being at Lantyan, they meant Castle Dore. In any case, Castle Dore was excavated in 1935. The fortress was shown to have been pre-Roman in origin but to have been refortified and occupied for about 200 years after the Romans withdrew. This makes it of about the correct date to have been the home of Mark. Not far away a seven foot tall monolith carries a broken inscription which records it to be the tombstone of a man named Drustanus – presumably the Drustan/Tristan of legend.

The earthworks of Castle Dore lie just off the B3269 and are fairly impressive. There is a complete inner circle of ditch and bank, and an outer circle that is only partially intact. Both survive today to a height of around 8ft, but would originally have been much larger and the ramparts topped by timber walls. During the time of Mark and Tristan, the interior contained a large timber hall 90ft long and 40ft wide with a row of wooden posts down its centre to support the roof. The floor was paved with stone – then a real luxury – and the building was approached by way of a porch. A second, similar building was 65ft by 30ft and there were other, smaller structures inside the defences.

A mile away stands the village of Golant with its church dedicated to St Sampson. The earliest versions of the story about Mark, Tristan and Iseult name the monastery of St Sampson as being only a short ride from the palace of King Mark. The geography fits the Castle Dore – Golant area. The dates fit as well. St Sampson was born in Wales in 486 and died in 560. He was Abbot of the monastery at Caldey from about 540 and used his authority to travel extensively through Wales, Dumnonia and Ireland. He is known to have founded a monastery at Golant at some point in these journeys, so it would have been in existence when King Mark ruled here in reality, though not in his legendary timescale as a contemporary of King Arthur. The reputed burial place of King Mark is at Carn Marth, on a hill just outside Redruth. Excavations found a few ashes that could not be properly dated, and nothing else.

Another legendary element of Cornish history that later became linked to King Arthur, for no apparent reason other than to share the fame of that ruler, is the Lost Land of Lyonesse. This vast stretch of countryside now lies beneath the waves between Cornwall and the Isles of Scilly. According to legend, Lyonesse was a rich and prosperous land of fertile plains that had several towns and 140 churches. One night a terrible storm arose that caused a cataclysmic flood. The sea came surging in to cover the land. The only survivor was a man named Trevelyan who happened to be awake at the time. He saw the waves coming, leapt on a white horse and galloped as hard as he could to Perranuthnoe, from where he watched the terrible disaster unfold.

The rocks of the Sevenstones, or Lethowsow, lie halfway between Cornwall and the Isles of Scilly. Richard Carew, writing in 1602, recorded that fishermen had brought up worked stones and pieces of window here. They declared that this proved the place to have been a town of Lyonesse. Other fishermen said that they sometimes heard bells tolling in the area as they were rolled about by the waves.

In Cornwall, the story of Lyonesse remained simply that of a land drowned at some vague date in the distant past. Mediaeval romancers, however, took it up. Like many other aspects of British legend they linked it to the story of King Arthur. In these versions Lyonesse was said to have been one of the richer parts of Arthur's realm. In different versions both Lancelot and Galahad are said to have come from Lyonesse. The land was drowned some years after Arthur's time.

The stories of Lyonesse seem to have grown out of a mix of fact and fancy. We know that the Isles of Scilly were one large island in around 250, but that they had become separated by around 950. The erosion of the islands continues, the island of Old Man being divided by the sea fairly recently. Rather older are the stone field walls revealed at low tide on the flats between Samson and Tresco, while the foundations of houses can be seen at low tide off St Martins.

Similar traces of drowned land can be seen in Mount's Bay, around St Michael's Mount. The old Cornish name for the Mount is Carrick Luzencuz, which translates as 'rock in the wood'. This must date back to the time when the bay was dry land, perhaps around 200BC. Off Marazion there is a fossilised forest. The tree stumps here are millions of years old, but so perfectly preserved that they could be mistaken for a recently drowned land. There are written records of extensive coastal flooding in the 12th century. It is probable that some coastal areas have been lost to the sea in the past 2,000 years or so, but that these have been small-scale losses. It seems likely that the memories of a few drowned fields and woods

The harbour of Mousehole. An attack on the town by the Spanish has entered local legend.

became conflated and embellished into the story of Lyonesse sometime around the time of the 12th-century floods. They were then taken up by romancers and merged into the Arthurian cycle of stories.

From the early 17th century comes the story of the fall of the House of Killigrew. The bare outlines of the story are well documented, but local gossip has it that the curse of a dying man lay behind the events. The Killigrews were one of the oldest of the great Cornish noble families, but not the most pleasant. They had a history of being quarrelsome and violent, as well as being willing to break the law of the land when it suited them to do so. Given their wealth, lands and connections there were few who dared oppose the Killigrews. There were too many dark lanes where a murderer's knife could be wielded.

In 1580 a pair of Hanseatic League ships from Germany took refuge from a storm in Falmouth Harbour. The locals put out in their boats, eager to make some money selling supplies to the visitors. Word was soon brought to Lady Jane Killigrew, who was in the family's town house at Falmouth at the time, that the ships carried a rich and valuable cargo bound for Spain. England was at peace with both Spain and the Hanseatic League at the time, but such a trifling matter did not deter Lady Killigrew. So far as she was concerned, Spain represented the hated Catholic enemy – this being the calm before the storm of the Spanish Armada. That made the cargo a legitimate target for plunder in the eyes of Lady Killigrew and many others.

Lady Killigrew mustered an armed mob and stormed the two ships. The cargo was plundered and taken ashore to be divided up. Lady Killigrew took two barrels of gold coins for her share. The two agents of the Spanish king, one on each ship, were bound hand and foot to be thrown overboard. As the first sank to his death, the second turned to Lady Killigrew.

'You may kill me now,' he shouted at her. 'But my blood will linger with you until my death is avenged by the extinction of your line.' Lady Killigrew spat her defiance, and the Spaniard was thrown to his doom.

Queen Elizabeth might have been able to turn a blind eye to plundering when it took place in the disputed waters off the Americas, but the plundering of neutral ships in an English harbour could not be ignored. Urged on by the ambassadors of both Spain and the Hanseatic League, Elizabeth acted. A force was sent to Cornwall. Several men were hanged on the Falmouth Harbour breakwater and Lady Jane Killigrew fled into exile in Ireland. She was sentenced to death in her absence and never returned home.

Lady Killigrew's son inherited the family wealth and estates, but he soon turned out to be a drunken dissolute who squandered the family wealth. His son was no better and the Killigrew acres shrank as they were sold off to pay the bills of gambling and drinking. By the time Lady Jane's great-grandson Sir George Killigrew inherited the family titles and estates he was left with little more than wealth than would suit a gentleman farmer. He had also inherited his father's and grandfather's wild ways.

In 1658 he was drinking in a tavern in Newlyn when he got into an argument with a lawyer named Walter Vincent. History does not record what the dispute was about, but it ended badly. Vincent taunted Killigrew that he was the descendant of gallow's bait, a reference to the death sentence passed on Lady Jane for her murder of the Spanish officials. Killigrew drew his sword, so did Vincent. The lawyer, being considerably less drunk, won the fight with ease and soon Sir George lay dead on the bar room floor. He left no male heirs, so the Killigrew name and titles became extinct, while the few acres of land left to the family passed through the female line to family of another name. As the doomed Spaniard had declared when he cursed Lady Jane, her family was wiped out because of the foul act done that day.

Another real event that has gained an accretion of legend is the Spanish raid of 1595. The historic event is fairly well documented. At dawn on 23 July four Spanish warships were sighted off Mousehole. The Spanish landed a small force which burned the town, then pushed inland for a mile or so to burn farms and loot anything they could find. The ships then moved on to Newlyn and Penzance, which were likewise pillaged and put to the torch.

The Cornish locals fled, but soon English warships were alerted and put out from Plymouth. By the time they had arrived the Spanish were gone. Only one man was killed, a resident of Mousehole called Jenkin Keigwin. He was felled by a cannonball shot from a Spanish ship before the landing began.

Before long, legend had got going. The unfortunate Jenkin Keigwin was turned into a local hero for his supposed defiance of the Spaniards. His tomb and the cannonball that killed him became objects of veneration. The ball was preserved at the Keigwin Arms inn, named after him, until the 19th century. A later story had it that the red cloaks worn by local fishwives had been mistaken by the Spaniards for soldiers' uniforms. The fright had caused them to flee Mousehole rather than march further inland. This latter tale is clearly a later invention. Red did not become the colour of English army uniforms until some 60 years after the raid. It does show, however, the way that a good story can become attached to a real event.

Another well documented event to have gathered legends quickly was the death of Admiral Sir Cloudesley Shovell in 1707. Shovell was, at the time, one of the most famous and most popular admirals in the fleet. He had joined the navy as a cabin boy in 1664 and gained command of his first ship aged only 19. He went on to fight the Dutch, French and Barbary Corsairs with great success. The highlight of his career was the capture of Gibraltar in 1704. He stayed with the Mediterranean fleet until October, when he was ordered home with most of his ships.

On 22 October, Shovell was leading his fleet from the Atlantic towards the Channel when a storm struck. Four of the ships were swept onto the Gill Stone off the Isles of Scilly. All four ships went down in minutes and some 2,000 men were drowned. A few

The Hurlers on Craddock Moor are linked to one of the better known incidents in Cornwall's legendary history.

survivors got ashore. Shovell was a rather portly chap, so his body floated and was found washing about in the surf of St Mary's by a search party sent out next day to look for survivors. The search was organised by Lord Berkeley, Shovell's second in command, who had taken over the rest of the fleet. The body was embalmed, then sent to lie in state in his London home before burial in Westminster Abbey.

So much for the facts. The legends began very quickly.

The first story to emerge was recorded in a Dutch newspaper only two months after the tragedy. According to this story, the body of Shovell had been found by local islanders before the search party had reached it. They had, the Dutch report ran, stolen an emerald ring from the body.

In 1736 Berkeley died a natural death. In 1790 it was recorded in a biography of Shovell written by his grandson Robert Romney that on his deathbed Berkeley handed over to his son a magnificent emerald ring. This ring had, it was said, been given to Berkeley when he visited the Isles of Scilly some years after the tragedy. He had been approached by a man and asked if he would visit the man's mother, who was dying in a cottage nearby. Berkeley had gone along to find an old woman. She gave him the ring and confessed that she had found Sir Cloudesley alive on the beach, but had strangled him and stolen the ring. She had then been overcome with remorse and had felt unable to sell the ring. She had kept it for years until she fell ill. She had been about to call the local vicar to confess her crime when she heard Lord Berkeley was nearby and so had sent for him instead. Having confessed, she died. Romney offered no proof of his story.

By the time folklorists were on the Isles of Scilly in the early 19th century, the story had grown further. It was now stated that the sole survivor of Shovell's own ship, HMS *Association*, had poured out a story when he reached land. This sailor had said that when the storm began an ordinary sailor had rushed up to Shovell to protest at the route being taken. The man was a native of Scilly and had warned Shovell that the course would lead to disaster. Shovell had pushed the man aside, but the man had then appealed to the crew not to follow such disastrous orders.

Shovell had then lost his temper and ordered the sailor to be hanged for mutiny and encouraging others to mutiny. The sailor had then turned on Shovell and recited to him Psalm 109, the notorious 'cursing psalm', which includes the lines 'Let his days be few and let another take his office. Let his children be fatherless and his wife a widow'. The hapless sailor had been strung up, then his body cut down and thrown overboard with a cannonball tied to his feet. The body had broken free of the ball and floated to the surface. It bobbed along in the wake of the *Association*, the pale, dead face staring at the ship until it struck the rocks and sank.

Shovell flung himself onto a wooden grating, which carried him ashore along with his favourite little dog. Both man and dog came ashore half drowned. A passing local man and his wife quickly killed Shovell for his ring and buried the body on the beach. The dog alerted the passing search party to the shallow grave, and the body was recovered. For all of this there was not the slightest shred of evidence. But the story of the stolen ring had begun very early on and refused ever to go away. Perhaps there was some truth in that at least.

Other historic legends in Cornwall are impossible to verify. They are set at no particular date and have no elements that allow the curious to try to trace them backwards. The story of the smuggler at Ralph's Cupboard is typical. This feature is now a deep cleft in the cliffs near Portreath where the roof of a cave has fallen in. It is said that the cave was named after a smuggler called Ralph who lived in it. He had an arrangement with a French ship that came and lay offshore so that Ralph could row out in his little boat to collect silk, brandy and other contraband. There is no clue as to when he lived, or if he was a real person at all.

Quite clearly more legendary than real are the various personages linked by local stories to the various prehistoric megaliths that stand around Cornwall. The Hurlers, for instance, stand on Craddock Moor. This is a complex of standing stones erected in the Bronze Age. There are three circles, one of 13 stones, one of 17 stones and one of 9 stones. Unlike many other stone circles of similar date, the Hurlers do not seem to be aligned on any particularly important astronomical event – such as midsummer sunrise or midwinter moonset, for instance. According to legend the Hurlers, as their name suggests, were men engaged in playing a game of hurling. This local Cornish sport was a rough and often violent contest between neighbouring villages. All the men of one village would play against all the men of another. The game began at a point midway between the two villages when a wooden ball was tossed into the air. The men would try to grab the ball and propel it back to their own village so that it would touch a 'goal', often the church doors or market cross. Pretty much anything was allowed – except for edged weapons – and injuries were frequent.

The hurlers of Craddock Moor, the old legend has it, decided to play their game on a Sunday when they should have been in church. No sooner had they begun than they all turned to stone. A broadly similar fate struck nine pretty young women from St Columb Major who followed a fiddler to dance up on the moors on a Sunday morning. All 10 were turned to stone the instant they began dancing when they should have been in church. The Nine Maidens stone circle, with a tall single monolith called The Fiddler, is the result. The same story is told of the Trippet Stones, a circle of 12 megaliths near Blisland.

CHAPTER 7

MYSTERIOUS GHOSTS

Cornwall is one of the most haunted counties in England. For any ghosthunter coming this way, it seems that there are more spooks and phantoms packed into the area than you could shake a stick at. Why this might be so is not entirely clear. Some suggest that it is the Celtic inheritance of the Cornish that predisposes them to play host to the ghosts of the past. Whether this is because ghosts prefer the Celts, or that the Celts are more credulous, depends on the opinions of the researcher. Others think that it is simply that the Cornish are more inclined to talk about their ghosts than folk elsewhere. Some say that the lively tourist industry has served to preserve and publicise old stories that might have been overlooked elsewhere.

Whatever the reason, there are ghosts in plenty. Some are more active than others. A few are more terrifying than the rest. The phantoms of Cornwall are a fairly mixed bunch of spectres. This chapter looks at various types of ghosts in an attempt to bring some sort of order to the vast number of hauntings that the county can boast.

HISTORIC GHOSTS

One of the most dramatic ghosts ever to be seen in Cornwall was the terrifying phantom that stormed across Bodmin Moor on 2 August in the year 1100. Riding over the moor on a hunting trip was Robert de Moreton, Earl of Cornwall. He was about to have a life-changing experience.

This Earl Robert was getting on in years, he may have been about 50 or so. He had been made Earl of Cornwall by William the Conqueror some 20 years earlier and given the task of holding down the area for the new king. So far as we know, Earl Robert never took the trouble to learn Cornish, but he employed men who could speak the local language. He enforced law and order at the point of his sword. If any locals felt inclined to rebel against the king who had won the crown in battle at Hastings in 1066, Earl Robert made sure that they took no action.

For all that he ruled well, Earl Robert was a brutal and ruthless man. Although appointed by William the Conqueror, he was always much closer to the son who would become William II. This William was nicknamed 'Rufus' because of his red hair and ruddy complexion. He was a bold and magnificent knight, a clever politician and a wily financier. He was also a drunken debauchee with a savage temper and a vicious ability to hold a grudge.

Earl Robert did not share all the gifts and sins of his lord king, but on one subject the two men were in absolute agreement. The Church was too powerful, too rich and too moralising to be tolerated. In modern parlance they viewed the bishops, abbots and monks as a bunch of politically correct do-gooders who needed putting in their place. Both King William and Earl Robert set out to do just that.

As soon as he heard that the younger William had become king, Earl Robert marched to the Priory of St Petroc and Bodmin backed by a troop of armed soldiers. The monks of St Petroc had particularly annoyed Earl Robert, and now he was having his revenge. Producing a sheaf of documents that the monks denounced as forgeries, Earl Robert declared that the lands of the monastery had only been loaned to St Petroc by the previous rulers of Cornwall. Now he was taking them back. The monks were thrown out and the wide, prosperous acres of the monastery were added to the estates of the earldom.

William Rufus did not hesitate either. Bishop William of Durham was declared an outlaw on trumped up charges of treason, but in reality because King William was fed up with his hectoring monologues urging the king to give up his wild ways. William followed this up by aping Earl Robert's actions and found excuses to strip monasteries and bishoprics of lands and wealth. If that did not annoy the Church enough, Rufus encouraged the Jews to conduct their businesses openly and with royal favour. He also blasphemed with a cheerful enthusiasm that shocked any churchman within hearing. When the Pope appointed a saintly and moralistic monk named Anselm to be Archbishop of Canterbury, William Rufus refused to allow him to enter England – then took all the rents due to the archbishopric to the royal coffers on the grounds that Anselm had not arrived to claim them. Men such as Earl Robert prospered.

Such was the situation when Earl Robert went out hunting that beautiful summer day. With his friends and servants, Earl Robert enjoyed the morning's hunt enormously. After the break for lunch a great red deer stag was spotted, and the hunters set off in pursuit. Earl Robert got separated from his colleagues and found himself alone on the moor. Then he spotted coming toward him a strange sight. At first he took it for a boy on a donkey, but as the thing came closer Earl Robert realised that it was a large black goat with a human body strapped to its back.

The goat came trotting up to the now rather disturbed Earl Robert. The body could now be seen to be that of King William Rufus, stripped naked and blackened as if by flames and fire.

'In the name of God and the Holy Trinity,' declared the shocked Earl Robert. 'What is this?'

The goat stopped, then eyed him coldly.

'I am the agent of the Devil,' it said. 'I have come to carry your king off to judgement. I was sent because St Alban complained to God of your master's evil deeds to Holy Mother Church. Beware I do not return for you.'

With that the goat turned and trotted off to vanish into a cleft in the rocks from which issued flames and the stench of sulphur.

Earl Robert rode home in stunned silence. He pushed past his hunting companions to pray in a small chapel. Then he sent a message off to King William asking for news. When the news came, it did not come from King William but from King Henry. William had died, the message said, due to a tragic hunting accident in the New Forest on 2 August and his younger brother Henry was now king.

Earl Robert hurried to pledge his oath of allegiance to the new king. Rumours that the hunting accident had been deliberate murder were rife at the time, and have continued to excite historians ever since. Nothing has been proved, but Henry was suspiciously ready to claim the throne, and had himself crowned just three days after William's death. Earl Robert was a changed man. He restored the estates of Bodmin, lavished money on the Church and gave up his blaspheming ways.

Such is the story that has come down to us. Some suspect that it is only a story. It was, after all, written down by monks who delighted in tales that showed the Church in a good light and which emphasised punishments for those who opposed its teachings. The fact remains, however, that Earl Robert did alter his behaviour. Some think it may have had more to do with his wish to please the new king than with any personal conversion following a demonic vision on Bodmin Moor. We will probably never know.

Almost as difficult to speak of with any certainty are the events that gave the name of Bodrugan's Leap to the great cliffs near Chapel Point, south of St Austell. The place is named after Sir Henry Bodrugan, whose family was one of the oldest and most respected in Cornwall. By 1485 the Bodrugan estates were vast and spreading – paying a reputed £10,000 in rent each year. If true, this would have made Sir Henry the richest man in Cornwall, after the Earl, and one of the wealthiest in England.

In June 1485 a message came to Cornwall from King Richard III. It stated that the notorious traitor Henry Tudor was preparing to invade England at the head of a French army and called on all loyal Englishmen to oppose him. In particular it ordered landowners, such as Bodrugan, to guard the ports and be ready to send a rider galloping to King Richard if the fleet of Henry Tudor was sighted. This was, of course, King Richard's take on the situation. The Wars of the Roses had by this date been raging on and off for almost 30 years. The Yorkist Edward IV had taken the throne from the Lancastrian Henry VI in 1461, lost it to Henry again in 1470 and finally won it back in 1471. He died in 1483 leaving the throne to his young son, Edward V. Exactly what happened next is uncertain.

Certainly the Bishop of Bath and Wells suddenly announced that the young king was illegitimate. Whether this was true or not is still the subject of debate, as is the problem of whether or nor the bishop acted alone or on the orders of others. Richard, brother to Edward IV and regent for Edward V, promptly executed Lord Hastings for treason and imprisoned the Archbishop of York as well as several other nobles and prelates. After two weeks of turmoil, rumour and unease, Richard announced that he accepted that his young nephew was, indeed, illegitimate. That made him king as Richard III. The former king Edward V and his younger brother were lodged in comfortable but very secure lodgings in the Tower of London, for which reason they became known as the Princes in the Tower.

The sudden accession of Richard to the throne was accepted by most of England, but not by everyone. Although King Henry VI and his son had both been killed in the Wars of the Roses, there was a Lancastrian claimant in the person of Henry Tudor. Henry was living in France, where the King of France was keeping him as a useful diplomatic tool in his intrigues against England. Hearing of Richard's taking of the throne, Henry went to work. He spread rumours that Richard had plotted the move all along, and that the lives of the Princes in the Tower were in danger. He made lavish promises to disaffected nobles and persuaded the King of France to lend him money to hire mercenaries. In the summer of 1485 his plans were complete, hence Richard's message to the gentry of Cornwall.

Sir Henry Bodrugan met with the other great landowners of southern Cornwall, Sir Richard Edgcumbe and Sir William Trevanion, to arrange their response. Between them the three men agreed to have the ports watched, to have messengers ready to ride and to prepare their men and weapons in case King Richard called them out to fight. Unknown to Bodrugan, however, Edgcumbe and Trevanion were secretly in league with Henry Tudor.

In August news came that Henry Tudor had landed in south Wales. Richard summoned all loyal Englishmen to join him at Leicester by 21 August to march against the rebel and his foreign mercenaries. Bodrugan called out his men, armed them and began the long march to Leicester. He never got there.

As Bodrugan and his men approached St Austell they saw the forces of Edgcumbe and Trevanion drawn up as if for battle blocking their way. Bodrugan sent a rider forward to ask his fellow landowners what they thought they were doing. The reply came back that they were holding the town for King Henry against the rebels of Richard of York. Bodrugan was furious at such treachery and ordered the attack.

There cannot have been more than a couple of hundred men on either side, but the battle was hard fought and bloody. The place where it happened was named Woeful Moor. The fight ended with defeat for Bodrugan. He rode south to his castle near what is now Bodrugan Barton, where he barricaded himself in. A few days later the news arrived that Richard had been killed at Bosworth Field and that Henry Tudor was now King Henry VII.

Bodrugan rode out to negotiate a surrender. Edgcumbe and Trevanion merely taunted him, saying he would be executed as a traitor. Rather than return to his castle and inevitable defeat, Bodrugan put his spurs to his horse and rode off to the east. The sea was less than a mile distant. Edgcumbe and Trevanion gave chase with their men, hoping to corner Bodrugan. They must have thought that they had him when they cut him off from Portmellon. In front of Bodrugan were now only the towering cliffs.

But Bodrugan did not draw rein or hesitate. He put his charger to gallop over the cliffs.

Man and horse soared through the air, tumbling down to splash into the sea far below. While Edgcumbe and Trevanion came to a halt on top of the cliffs, Bodrugan bobbed back to the surface. He swam to a fishing boat waiting nearby and clambered aboard. He then turned to shake his fist at his one-time friends and cursed them roundly for their treason. Then he handed a purse of coins to the fisherman and ordered him to set sail for France.

Edgcumbe and Trevanion divided up Bodrugan's lands between them. They thus gained greatly from their support for the new king. Bodrugan spent the rest of his life abroad, earning a living as a soldier of fortune. The cliffs from which he made his spectacular escape became known as Bodrugan's Leap. It is said that on certain days a ghostly knight is seen riding hell for leather out of Bodrugan's Barton to disappear over the 50ft high cliffs of Bodrugan's Leap. It seems that, unable to return in life, Sir Henry Bodrugan returns in death to his ancestral acres.

Another period of civil strife has left its ghostly mark on Braddock Down, south of Lostwithiel. When the English Civil War broke out between King Charles I and his Parliament, Cornwall declared for the king. The move was important since it delivered to the Royalist cause not only the county treasury, but also the flow of taxes levied on tin exports. Sir Ralph Hopton did a fine job of mustering and arming Cornishmen for service, but he was chronically short of both artillery and cavalry.

In January 1643 the Parliamentarians invaded Cornwall, hoping to secure the tin wealth for their cause. The invasion came in two prongs. The Scot Colonel Ruthven led 4,000 men out of Plymouth to march south of Bodmin Moor. A second army of about 5,000 men under the Earl of Stamford was invading north of Bodmin Moor. Stamford and Ruthven intended to meet at Bodmin, then tackle Hopton's army, which lay at Truro. With only 5,000 men available once fortresses and ports had been garrisoned, Hopton knew he had to tackle the Roundheads before they could meet. He decided to take on Ruthven first.

The two armies met on Braddock Down on the morning of 19 January. Hopton had only two light cannon, while Ruthven had a dozen heavier pieces that he had dragged from Plymouth. As Hopton was drawing up his army, with the infantry in the centre and dragoons and cavalry on the wings, he realised that Ruthven's cannon were nowhere in sight. They were, in fact, at the rear of the Parliamentarian column, as Ruthven had not expected to fight before reaching Bodmin. Deciding to attack before the enemy cannon could be got into action, Hopton ordered his men forward.

The Cornish infantry advanced in perfect order, drove off an attack by Roundhead cavalry and plunged into the centre of Ruthven's line. The battle did not last long. Not yet properly in formation, the Parliamentarian infantry collapsed and fled. The pursuit continued all the way to the gates of Lostwithiel. Hopton captured all Ruthven's cannon as well as over a thousand prisoners. He then turned north, but Stamford retreated as soon as he heard of Ruthven's defeat. Cornwall remained in Royalist hands and Hopton went on the

Braddock Down was the scene of a bloody battle during the Civil War of the 1640s, and the ghosts of the slain return to haint the field.

offensive. He got as far as Bath before Royalist defeats elsewhere forced him to retreat to Cornwall.

The ghosts that lurk at Braddock Down are presumably those of the men killed here. They are the phantoms of men on foot wearing helmets and trailing pikes. The ghosts trudge in disconsolate fashion over the fields and down the lanes. Their shoulders are stooped, their heads bent down. Those who have seen them report an overwhelming feeling of tiredness and sadness as the ghosts pass by.

The Civil War left another spectral hangover at Godolphin House, near Penzance. In the later stages of the Civil War, King Charles sent his son and heir, the later King Charles II, to Cornwall. It was believed that he would be safer being looked after by Lord Hopton and his steady Cornish infantry than if he stayed at the royal court in Oxford. The young prince was only a teenager, but he was already beginning to show the jovial nature and eye for the ladies that would later earn him the nickname of the Merry Monarch.

Charles spent much of his time at Godolphin House. One of the rooms was adapted for his use. It was provided with a hiding place and with a secret passage leading to the gardens. As the war turned against the Royalists, Roundhead troopers with orders to capture the prince began to scour the countryside and nobody could be certain when they would reach Godolphin House. That room is haunted by Charles to this day. He is seen only from outside the house, staring out of a window, and never from inside. Interestingly he appears as a fully mature man, more as he would have been when he died than when he lived here. Perhaps his spirit has chosen to return here to live out some happy days.

One of the most famous ghosts in Cornwall is that of the unfortunate Dorothy Dingle who appears at Botathan, near Launceston. In the summer of 1665 young Dorothy was being courted by John Bligh. Both youngsters came from local farming families and the romance was welcomed by the two families. Then Dorothy Dingle died suddenly. A few days later John Bligh announced that he had got a job with a distant relative some miles away and promptly left Botathan. There was some local gossip that Dorothy had been pregnant and that her death had been linked to her condition. There was, however, no suggestion of foul play and the two families remained on good terms.

Three years after the death, Henry Bligh, John's younger brother, saw the ghost of Dorothy. He was walking to school in Petherwin and, although his age is not given in the record, he was presumably under 10. Unsurprisingly, the sight of the apparition shook the boy considerably. He saw the ghost a second time a few days later. This time he remained calm and watched it. The spectre walked towards him, then passed him by, heading towards Botathan with its eyes fixed on the horizon. The phantom showed no signs of having seen the boy at all.

Young Henry went to see his father, who in turn took him to see the Revd John Rudall, vicar of Launceston, who had a reputation for being open minded on such matters. Rudall questioned the boy closely and accepted that he had indeed seen a ghost. Rudall took the time to visit Botathan and on one trip he too saw the ghost. He had intended to challenge the ghost in the name of God, but his courage failed him and he fled. Rudall later regretted his lack of courage and decided that he had to do something about the ghost. He went to see his bishop to obtain permission for an exorcism. Having got the agreement of the bishop, Rudall then read up all he could on the subject. After some weeks he felt ready to face the phantom.

Rudall went back to Botathan armed with a Bible, a wand cut from a rowan tree and a list of instructions that he had copied out from old volumes on exorcism. Finding the place where he had seen the ghost, Rudall drew a circle on the ground with his rowan twig, then drew a pentacle within the circle and finally pushed the rowan wand into the ground at the design's centre. Standing over the wand he began summoning the spirit of the dead woman in Syriac. He chose this ancient language as one of the documents he had consulted assured him that all spirits understood the tongue. After a few minutes the ghost appeared. Rudall asked her why she was walking the fields and lanes around her old home. The ghost replied that she had committed a sin when alive for which she had never sought forgiveness. She confessed her act to Rudall, who assured her that she would be forgiven by God's grace. The ghost then vanished.

That is the version of the story that Rudall told some years later to his friend, the novelist Daniel Defoe. Defoe wrote the events up as a short story which proved to be hugely popular. There is one problem with the story as retold by Rudall. According to him he laid the ghost, but she continues to walk. The phantom has not been seen as often in recent years as in the past, so perhaps her strength is waning. When she does appear, however, she is seen walking with confident stride toward Botathan, her old home. It is to be hoped that if Rudall did not bring her soul peace, then it shall soon find it.

The church of St Bartholomew at Warleggan stands in an isolated position up a lane outside the village on the slopes that lead up to Bodmin Moor. It is a charming little church of 13th-century date that was extended in 1480. Other than a few repairs it has barely changed since. The round churchyard seems to have been a burial ground since around the year 600. Just outside the church door is an ancient stone cross that might be eighth century in date. It did not always stand here, but once marked the path over a shoulder of Bodmin Moor to Temple. The two villages belonged to the same parish, so the rectors of Warleggan often walked the path to preach at Temple. It became known as a holy path, a reputation perhaps enhanced by the ancient cross.

In 1901 the then rector, the Revd C.E. Lambert, held a service at Warleggan, then set off to walk to Temple. He never got there. Those waiting for the service finally set off along the holy path to look for him. His body was found slumped on the ground. It was presumed that he had died of a heart attack.

It is not the ghost of the unfortunate Revd Lambert that haunts the church and the holy path, but that of the altogether stranger Revd Frederick Densham, who was rector here from 1931 to 1953. The Revd Densham of Warleggan is usually described

The ancient cross at Warleggan that formerly stood on the high moor behind the church.

The lane that leads to the church at Warleggan is haunted by the ghost of the Revd Frederick Densham, who was rector here from 1931 to 1953.

in books as being 'eccentric', but that does not even begin to describe his actions as recorded in local gossip and stories. It must be admitted that the Revd Densham got off to a bad start with his parishioners. He was a strict vegetarian at a time when such a thing was unheard of in a remote rural community like Warleggan. He also banned the village pigeon shoot, previously a very popular social event, on the grounds that it was cruel to pigeons. He then redecorated the Rectory in the brightest primary colours and gave Biblical names to the rooms and garden features.

Although a knowledge of scripture and passion for the Bible are generally considered good things in a clergyman, Densham took it to extremes. He would speak to his parishioners in Biblical references. Meeting a man on a rainy day he might nod then say 'I Kings 18:41' before passing on. The puzzled local would have to consult his Bible to learn that the relevant verse reads 'And Elijah said unto Ahab, Get thee up, eat and drink; for there is a sound of abundance of rain'.

Densham was very well educated and widely travelled, and it may have been that the small, remote parish in which he found himself was not to his taste. He was 63 when he arrived, and his eccentricities became more pronounced as he grew older. He would set up life-sized cardboard cutouts of people to swell the numbers of his congregation at services. Cards were set out reserving seats for past rectors of the parish from centuries gone by. He would hold services at unusual times of day, and go through the entire ritual even if nobody turned up. His disputes with the Parish Council became famous. The local press carried frequent stories about disagreements over the colours of chairs to be used at meetings, when the heating in the church should be put on and how services should be conducted. Some of the more pronounced eccentricities of Warleggan's rector even made it into *Life* magazine in the US.

That said, there is no doubt that Densham was a most conscientious clergyman. He did not miss a single Sunday morning service, even when he was on his annual official holiday. He made great efforts to make the church and services more appealing to children, and installed a playground outside the church. When he died he left the diocese £1500, then a substantial sum of money, to buy cars for clergymen with large rural parishes to serve. Clearly Densham loved Warleggan, despite his oddness and frequent disputes. It is no wonder that his ghost returns to potter about the churchyard and the lane that leads to it. It is a beautiful little church. Like so many in Cornwall it is well worth a visit, and visitors are urged to leave a small cash gift to help meet the spiralling costs of maintenance.

MARITIME GHOSTS

Cornwall is surrounded on three sides by the sea. The men of Cornwall have for centuries gone to sea to fish, trade, fight and otherwise seek their fortunes. It is no wonder that so many of the phantoms of the county are linked to the oceans.

One of the oldest of these ghosts is the one that lurks just out to sea off Boscastle. The lovely church of Forrabury stands on a headland overlooking the harbour. Strangely the church has no bells, the result of a terrible disaster that occurred hundreds of years ago. The good folk of Forrabury, when their church was completed, found the money to pay for a

The seas off Boscastle echo to the sounds of phantom bells.

fine peal of bells. They were determined to have the best in Cornwall, so they sent to a famous foreign foundry for the work to be done.

After some months the bells were ready and one of the local fishermen was sent out to act as pilot to ensure the safe arrival of the valuable cargo. The voyage home went without incident and soon the ship with the bells was hove to off Boscastle waiting for the tide to turn so that she could sail in. Just then the bells of Tintagel church rang out for Sunday service. The fisherman went down on his knees to pray to God and give thanks for a safe voyage.

The ship's captain cuffed him round the head, sending him sprawling to the deck.

'You don't want to go thanking God for that voyage,' he laughed. 'It was my skills as a seaman that got us here. And don't you forget it when these bells are landed and it is time to pay me.'

The fisherman was aghast at the captain's words and only prayed the harder. The captain laughed even louder and began mocking the man's faith. That was when a great wave began to loom up out of the Atlantic, far to the west. The wave came on quickly and remorselessly. By the time the sacrilegious captain saw it coming, it was too late. The ship was overwhelmed and sent to the bottom of the sea. The only survivor was the fisherman, who managed to scramble ashore on the rocks at the base of the cliffs at Forrabury.

Ever since the sound of ghostly bells has tolled out from beneath the waves off Boscastle Harbour to herald an approaching storm. All the local fishermen know the sound and hurry back to harbour rather than risk sharing the watery grave of that foreign captain. Some say that the bell ship returns in phantom form at the height of storms to ride the waves along this stretch of coast. If seen, she is to be avoided. The captain seeks only to lure others to join him.

Ghostly bells of a very different kind have been heard ringing over Mount's Bay, along with a phantom voice calling out 'I will, I will'. This is all that is left of a handsome young sailor known locally as Yorkshire Jack, from the county of his birth. Back in the 18th century, Yorkshire Jack came to live at Marazion. He sailed with the ships that plied their trade between Cornwall and Brittany and soon became popular, with his cheerful disposition and good looks. It was his misfortune to fall into an affair with a pretty woman called Sarah Polgrain from nearby Ludgvan. The problem was that Sarah was married to a wealthy but elderly farmer. Sarah and Yorkshire Jack were accustomed to meet in the churchyard on days when his ship was in. If old man Polgrain was out, they would retire to Sarah's house, but otherwise would find a quiet spot in the nearby woods for their lovemaking. The affair jogged along for a while, then old man Polgrain died. The death did not really surprise anyone as the elderly man had been suffering ill health for some time.

After a decent interval Sarah Polgrain and Yorkshire Jack announced their engagement. The wedding day was set for a year after Sarah's first husband's death for decency's sake, but the couple moved in together at once to live as husband and wife in Marazion.

It was sheer chance that they should be walking along arm in arm when a carriage passed by carrying an apothecary from Truro on his way to business in Penzance. The apothecary recognised Sarah as a woman to whom he had sold a quantity of arsenic, although then she had been accompanied by an elderly husband, not a dashing young lover. He asked about her, learned of her husband's convenient death and took his suspicions to the magistrates. Sarah Polgrain was arrested, tried and convicted of murder. She was hanged just a few weeks before her planned wedding day.

Yorkshire Jack was absolved of any guilt, but he lost his cheerful demeanour. He moped about Marazion, shunned the company of other youngsters and went about his work in morose silence. He confessed to a sailor friend of his that worked the same trade to Brittany that he was being followed about by Sarah's ghost. The friend suggested he should go to see the local vicar, or perhaps the doctor, but Jack did neither.

One the day of the planned wedding, Yorkshire Jack was on board a ship returning from Brittany. He was off duty as the ship put into Mount's Bay. Several of the sailors heard the sound of footsteps, unmistakably those of somebody wearing high heels. They went down the passageway to the cabin where Jack was resting. Seconds later Jack came up on deck, moving like one in a trance.

'She has come to marry me,' he muttered. He turned to look at a person who was invisible to everyone else on board. 'Yes,' he called out quite loudly. 'I will, I will.' With that Jack sprang to the bulwarks and vaulted over the side into the sea. As his body sank beneath the waves the sounds of church bells echoed over the waters as if ringing out for a wedding. The phantom bells and voice have been heard many times over the years.

Another tragic love story lies behind the haunting of Porthgwarra, also known as Sweetheart's Cove. The ghosts seen here are those of a young couple, strolling along the water's edge arm in arm and obviously besotted by each other. Some time in the 1840s Nancy, daughter of a well-to-do local farmer, fell in love with a penniless fishing lad named William. Nancy's father disapproved and told William in no uncertain terms that he would not allow his daughter to marry a pauper, then he banned William from visiting. Undeterred, William pledged that he would go to sea to seek his fortune, returning to marry Nancy once this had been achieved. He went off to Plymouth, signed on with a merchant ship and left.

Convinced that he would be back soon, Nancy took to climbing up to the cliffs above Hella Point to keep a watch for his ship. She spent so much time there that the place became known as Nancy's Garden. Weeks became months, months became years and no word came from the absent William. Still Nancy mooned about, refusing to so much as look at the young men who came calling. Gradually the fair Nancy went mad with waiting for her lost love.

One night, she came tearing down from her room dressed in a fine gown and her overcoat. She blurted out to her father that William had at last come for her. He was rich and ready to marry her. The astonished father looked around for some sign of the returning sailor, but there was none. Nancy said that he had knocked on her window and instructed her to come down to Porthgwarra Bay to meet him. Pushing aside her family, the girl ran out into the night.

That same evening, William's father had a knock at the door. Outside stood his son. William told his father that he had made his fortune and had come back to marry Nancy. Then he turned and walked off. The father tried to follow him, but lost him in the darkness. He then made his way over to Nancy's house just in time to find her father setting out in search of his daughter. Together the two men hurried down to Porthgwarra Cove, but they were unable to find any sign of either William or Nancy. Months later a letter came to William's family. It had been written from Plymouth by a sailor. It told them that he had been on board a ship in the Indian Ocean with William. A terrific storm had blown up quite suddenly and William had been swept overboard and drowned. The grieving family sent word to Nancy's family. Only then did they realise that the day on which William had died was the day when he had been seen by both his father and Nancy. The body of neither young lover was ever found, but their ghosts stroll the beach in apparent happiness.

A rather less dramatic tale of a death being announced by a ghost comes from Gwinnear. In 1892 a lady living here received a telegram announcing the death by shipwreck of the

The Finnygook Inn at Crafthole takes its name from the ghost that haunts the area.

young sailor to whom her daughter was engaged. Wanting to break the news as gently as possible, the woman went up to her daughter's bedroom. She knocked and entered to find her daughter in tears.

'I know what you have come to say,' said the younger woman. 'My darling has been here already and told me for himself. He was half-dressed in his shirt and trousers, but one brace only over his shoulder and missing a boot.' When a letter arrived giving fuller details of the tragedy than the telegram it included a description of the body as it had been washed ashore. It was dressed exactly as the girl had said.

A rather different sailor haunts the Finnygook Inn at Crafthole, and the road from Portwrinkle. This is the spectre of Silas Finny, who ran a gang of smugglers based here in the 1790s. The criminal enterprise prospered and all seemed set fair, until one fatal night in 1793 when the gang was expecting a particularly important cargo of brandy and lace to be landed at Whitsand Bay. A disagreement flared up over how the cargo should be sold on. The details of the dispute have been lost, but it was severe enough for Finny to be deposed as leader and, indeed, to be thrown out of the gang altogether.

Finny was not a man to take such a thing calmly. He slipped away on a pretext and hurried to the headquarters of the revenue men in Plymouth. When the cargo was being landed the revenue men pounced, rounding up the entire gang. The smugglers were convicted and sentenced to transportation to Australia. The sentence was a harsh one as the authorities were trying to crack down on smuggling at the time. Finny got paid a handsome reward and thereafter returned to his more usual profession as a fisherman.

Some years later Captain William Bligh took over as the governor in Australia. He had previously become famous both as an officer under the explorer Captain Cook and as the luckless captain of HMS *Bounty* when the well-known mutiny on that ship took place. Despite his reputation for being an awkward man with a quick temper, Bligh was more humane than most governors of the penal colony. He encouraged his prisoners to found farms and trade on their own account. Taking advantage of this, several of the smugglers who had served out their sentences were able to earn enough money to pay for the passage home to Britain.

It was not long after this that Silas Finny was found lying dead on the road from Portwrinkle, where he kept his ship, to Crafthole where he lived. Nobody doubted that he had been murdered by one of the men he had betrayed, but there was no evidence to bring any of them to justice.

Soon Finny began to walk again. He wandered the road where he had been killed, and was particularly fond of hanging around the New Inn. This was where he had based his gang and where he had been a regular customer while his former colleagues were in Australia. So often was the ghost seen that the New Inn was renamed the Finnygook Inn – gook being a local word for ghost. The phantom walks still, and some locals will not walk down the haunted road past midnight.

Another smuggler, this time from Mullion, had a most disturbing experience one night in 1795. He had been unable to join his comrades on a trip over to Brittany to pick up a load of brandy due to having to take care of some business in Helston. His business concluded, he was walking home and had got as far as Hulzephron Cliff when he saw a group of men approaching. He was amazed to see that they were his shipmates marching along in total silence. The men did not give him so much as a glance, but tramped on past. He learned later that the ship had foundered and all drowned that very day.

An altogether more respectable sailor haunts the Dolphin Inn at Penzance. Known locally as the Captain, this ghost seems to date from the 18th century judging by his long coat with brass buttons and embroidered buttonholes. He is heard much more often than he is seen. The captain always patrols the same route. He starts at an upstairs window overlooking the front of the building, then leaves that room to walk along the corridor and down the stairs, near the bottom of which he vanishes.

Whoever he may have been, the Captain of the Dolphin was nowhere near as important in life as the man whose ghost haunts the old manor house at Veryan. This house was built around 1580 by the Kempe family, and it was here that Arthur Kempe was born. As a young man Kempe sailed with Captain Cook on his famous voyages of discovery to the Pacific

Ocean. He later rose to become an admiral, though his period of high command came only after the great naval victory over the French and Spanish at Trafalgar in 1805 ensured that the Royal Navy had no serious rivals left to fight. He died in 1823, leaving his house and all it contained to his widow.

The ghost of this venerable naval admiral appears as he was in his years of retirement. He has grey hair and a figure rather fuller than it must have been during his active years of command at sea. He wears a long blue coat with cutaway front and brass buttons, such as an admiral would wear when on duty. He is seen standing quietly in the hall or dining room. Interestingly the phantom will be seen by one person, while a second in the same room can see nothing unusual. On one occasion a guest at the house felt a heavy hand fall on his shoulder while at dinner, but on turning round there was nobody there. Presumably he had been touched by the ghostly admiral.

The ghostly lady of Sennen Cove did not live long enough to enjoy a retirement like that of Admiral Kempe. Nobody knows her name, so she is called simply the Irish Woman. She is the phantom of the sole survivor of an Irish bark that went down in Sennen Cove during a storm. This unfortunate woman managed to swim to a rock some distance offshore and dragged herself out of the waves. The storm was so fierce, however, that nobody could put out in a boat to go to her rescue. For hours she clung to her rock before exhaustion did its work and she lost her grip to be washed away to her death.

The offshore rock at Sennen Cove is haunted by a most unfortunate Irish woman.

The ghostly Irish Woman is still seen from time to time. She appears to be clinging to the rock where she died while waves break over her. It is, those who have seen her report, a heartbreaking sight. Another fatality haunts the beach at Gwithian. This is the phantom of a smuggler who drowned here some two centuries ago. The exact circumstances of his death are in dispute. Some say he committed suicide after his beloved sister died, others that he was drowned landing a cargo of contraband. Still others say that he was killed in a fight with the Revenue men. Everyone agrees that he was a smuggler, however, and that his ghost returns when a north wind is blowing.

Very definitely not a smuggler is the ghostly sailor of Quay Street in Penzance. This local man went to sea to seek his fortune and ended up some years later as a trader in India making a great deal of money from trade. He eventually gave up his position to come home to Penzance to retire. He bought a house on Quay Street and made contact with his family, who had long since given him up for dead. A few weeks later he vanished. His family said he had gone back to India, but few people believed that he would have given up his retirement plans. When his ghost was seen pacing Quay Street, murder was suspected. His family fled. The hapless sailor's body was found later, hidden beneath the floor of the house. Presumably his family had murdered him for his cash. Sadly, they were never brought to justice, and perhaps that is why the dead man's ghost still walks.

One sea spectre that is curiously out of place is the phantom lugger of Croft Pasco Pool. This large pond is located high on the Goonhilly Downs of the Lizard Peninsula. This lugger was seen many times in the 1870s and 1880s. Usually observed only by moonlight, it appeared to be rocking back and forth on the waves with its lugsails set, but failing to catch any wind. There does not seem to have been any story attached to this odd phantom, but it was reported often enough.

In 1881 the folklorist Robert Hunt was travelling through Cornwall collecting material when he heard of the phantom lugger of Croft Pasco Pool. He went up to the pool and could see no way that a lugger — real or ghostly — could ever get there. He was staying in Helston and that evening made the mistake of voicing his opinion that the ghostly lugger was nothing more than a white horse seen standing in the shallows of the pool at dusk. One of the drinkers in the inn that evening had himself seen the ghostly ship. He gave his opinion of Hunt's idea firmly, and was backed up by the other locals so vociferously that Hunt thought it prudent to retire to his room.

A rather mysterious phantom ship has been seen sailing into Porthcurno. It is not content merely to enter the harbour, but will then take to the air and sail inland toward Trethewey. According to a legend recorded in the later 19th century, this ghost ship was linked to a local family called Martin who lived at Chygwidden Farm, since demolished. It seems that Mr Martin senior was a drunken brute who beat his son. When Mr Martin married a new wife, Young Martin went to sea rather than stay at home. The years passed. First Mr Martin died, then his wife. As nothing had been heard of Young Martin it was presumed that he had either died or was never coming home. The property passed to cousins – a brother and sister named Kevin and Eleanor.

Then Young Martin came back from the sea, landed at Porthcurno and walked inland to Chygwidden Farm. He brought with him a swarthy foreigner whom he called José, a pet dog and several large chests. Kevin and Eleanor at once offered to leave, but Young Martin declined the offer. He asked only that a room be kept ready for himself and José to use whenever they came home. From his chests he extracted fine silks and jewels for Eleanor and gold coins for Kevin. He then used more gold coins to have built a fine, sleek hoy – a type of small sailing craft used for coastal trade.

He and José would often put to sea in the hoy. Sometimes they were gone for a day or two, at other times for months on end. All sorts of rumours circulated about where they went and what they did, but nobody really knew. After some years of this, Young Martin fell ill. As he lay dying at Chygwidden Farm, he made José and his cousin promise that he would not be buried in the same churchyard as his hated father. They carried him down to the hoy. José put to sea with the body, accompanied by Eleanor and the pet dog. Kevin stayed on shore, returning to Chygwidden Farm.

Some days later a great storm arose, battering Porthcurno with gigantic waves. The hoy was seen heading in toward the small harbour, braving the tempest. On deck could be seen three figures, one of them a woman, and a dog. The boat reached the harbour, but then floated up into the air and raced on inland as if blown by the wind. It came to Chygwidden Farm, where it hovered for a while, then veered off and vanished.

Ever since that awful day, the ghostly hoy of Porthcurno has been seen coming in against the tide and wind as dusk draws in. It takes to the air and sails inland for a mile or so before it vanishes.

Another ghostly sailing vessel has been seen putting into St Levan, then taking to the air and moving half a mile or so inland. This time it is a proper three-masted, square-rigged ship that is seen, not a small hoy. What ship it might be is unknown, but some think that it may be linked in some way to the tomb of Captain Richard Wetherall, which lies in the churchyard. Wetherall was the commander of the brig *Aurora* from the Isles of Scilly that was wrecked off nearby Gwennap Head in 1811. As the ship foundered, Wetherall ordered his crew to take to the boat. For some reason, he turned back as if to fetch something and a great wave parted the boat from the ship. Seeing that he was doomed, Wetherall waved to his crew then went back to the place where he was accustomed to stand and rang eight bells on the ship's bell to signify the end of his watch. Then the brig went down, taking its captain with it.

When Wetherall's body was recovered it was buried in St Levan's churchyard. His family later sent the money to pay for his impressive tomb. It is said that at midnight on the

Talland Bay is the haunt of the mystery ship known as the Jack Harry.

anniversary of his death a phantom bell sounds out eight bells from the tomb. Some might think the ghostly ship to be that of Captain Wetherall, but his was a two-masted brig and the phantom has three masts.

One stormy day in the 18th century a ship in obvious distress put into St Ives Bay. It was a fine, big, three-masted merchant ship that had obviously been badly battered by the storm. The rigging was hanging loose, the sails were torn to shreds and the crew were firing off distress rockets while desperately working the pumps. The locals gathered to watch, while some of the braver fishermen manned one of their larger boats and put out to effect a rescue. The storm was terrible, but the bay waters were slightly sheltered. The fishing boat began to work its way out to the stricken ship.

Suddenly the ship was gone. It had not gone down or left, but had simply vanished into thin air. Puzzled and worried, the fishermen turned back to shore. They had just got back on dry land when the mystery ship appeared again. Exactly as before, it floundered into the bay firing off distress rockets and with its crew working the pumps. Not sure what to make of the return of the disappearing ship, the men stood and stared.

Then the mystery ship began to settle deeper into the water. The St Ives people realised that this time it was a real ship. They hurried back to the fishing boat. Suddenly a great snap was heard and the mysterious ship broke in half before sinking. There were no survivors. Divers subsequently visited the wreck when the storm had abated and found that she was the *Neptune*, a merchant ship from London bound for India.

The ghostly *Neptune* has been seen many times since. Always she comes into St Ives Bay during a storm, firing off distress rockets and with her sails in tatters. Then she just vanishes.

A rather different ship is to be seen in Talland Bay off Porthallow. This is the *Jack Harry*. Like the ghost ship of St Ives, the *Jack Harry* was not at first recognised for what it was. One day, apparently in the 1750s though the records are not clear, a ship was seen off the coast in Talland Bay. There was a moderate gale blowing and a steep sea running. The conditions were nothing too awful, but the ship seemed to be in some difficulty and was in danger of foundering. Fishermen put off from Looe and Polperro to try to rescue the people on board. Try as they might to reach the stricken vessel, the fishermen could not do so. Just as they approached the wind and waves would move it out of reach again.

Finally a boat from Looe managed to draw up close and a fisherman threw a rope to the men and women on board, but the rope just fell straight through the ship, which then vanished. Only then did the Looe men realise that they had got into a dangerous position on a lee shore. With difficulty they got to safety. The locals concluded that the ship had been sent by the Devil to lure innocent seamen on to dangerous rocks. Thereafter the ghost ship of Talland Bay was seen frequently. Sometimes it seemed to be in trouble, at other times to be running well. But it always sought to lure other ships to follow it into danger before abruptly vanishing. The locals dubbed it the *Jack Harry* and gave it a wide berth.

Even worse than the *Jack Harry* is the Death Ship of Tregeseal. This small ship is seen cruising off the coast with black sails and a black hull. It is said to date back to a funeral that took place in around 1740. A local man lay sick of fever and sent a message for the vicar to visit him. When the vicar arrived, the man poured out a most terrible story. He had left the village when a young man and for some years lived a life of crime and utmost depravity in Bristol. Murder, rape and theft had been his occupations for years. Now the man feared that he was dying and was terrified of the fate that awaited him. The vicar did his best to console the man, but felt it his duty to tell the man that it was up to God's mercy what fate would befall a soul so mired in sin. The sick man then begged to be buried in a sealed lead coffin on the very day that he died. The vicar agreed.

The next day the man died, and as he had wished he was hurriedly sealed into a lead coffin. As the funeral procession wound out toward the church an ominous black ship with black sails came nosing into Tregeseal. It hove to off the shore. Then a mighty voice boomed out 'The time has come, but not the man', then it sailed away. It still sometimes stands into Tregeseal or sails past. If the voice booms out a local death is certain within the next few days.

TRANSPORT GHOSTS

Spectral forms of transport have a long and honourable history. The most famous type of ghostly transport is the phantom coach, and Cornwall has more than its share of those rattling around the lanes and highways. But the roads are haunted by more modern forms of spectre as well.

Take the Tehidy Road just outside Camborne, for instance. Along this stretch of road has been seen a spectral lady on a bicycle. There is nothing particularly unusual about the ghost, except for her ghostly status. She is simply a middle-aged lady in a grey cardigan with a hat on her head riding a bicycle. It is only when she vanishes into thin air that those who encounter her realise that there is anything unusual about her at all.

Another cycling ghost is to be encountered just outside Zennor. The lane leading to Foage Farm is haunted by man on a bike. He is dressed in a jacket with a round neck and a cloth cap, both of which seem to date him to the mid-Victorian period. His face and clothes are spattered with blood. It has been speculated that he may be the ghost of a miner who was killed at the Rosevale Mine by an underground explosion.

Not quite a ghostly vehicle, but closely related, are the 'funny goings-on' around Luxulyan. Starting in around 2000 and continuing to this day, there has been a series of odd road accidents near the hilltop village. One car passing over Black Hill experienced four punctures simultaneously. When the startled driver got out to investigate there was nothing on the road that could have caused the damage, yet all four tyres had blown out. A van leaving the village suddenly veered off the road into a hedge. The driver reported that it felt as if the

A cycling ghost haunts the lane outside Zennor that leads to Foage Farm.

steering wheel had been yanked out of his hands. The locals at first blamed the incidents on a group of witches. They were not local followers of Wicca, but a group of townies come in from outside the area to use the woods down in the valley. Locals reported finding dolls stuck with pins and other occult objects hanging from the trees.

A police spokesman confirmed that there had been a spate of road traffic accidents in recent years, some of which could not readily be explained, and certainly more than would normally be expected in a quiet area like this. 'But,' the spokesman went on, 'traffic flow has been up sharply because of the Eden Project, which might account for it.'

Rather more dramatic is the ghost coach of Lanreath. This spectacular visitation is usually seen running along Bridle Lane, through the village and past the church. There are various stories about this phantom coach. One has it that the four horses that pull it are all headless, as is the driver. Another tale says that the driver is a demon who seeks to lure people on board with the promise of a lift to their destination, only to carry them off to Hell. A lady speaking in 2004, who had seen the coach a few years earlier, said 'It is a black coach pulled by six headless horses and gallops through the village late at night. As it passes, the pounding hooves and wheels make the windows rattle, which is why that there lane is called Rattle Lane. It comes down the hill, past the church and then gallops out of the village again. Very dramatic and frightening it is too.'

The lane haunted by the ghost coach of Lanreath.

The ghost coach of Penryn has a similar power to carry off unwary locals and take them to Hell. In this case it is not necessary to be fooled into climbing aboard. The driver himself is more than capable of grabbing anyone he fancies and dragging them into his fatal vehicle. The best advice is to hide out of sight and hope that the ghost coach goes rattling by. Another phantom coach is said to trundle through the streets of Penzance. This conveyance can be fatal to those who meet it, but only if it stops. If it passes by then the witness has been spared. The ghost coach of St Ives similarly passes through the streets of the town and is best avoided.

Wadebridge is said to have two phantom coaches, though some suspect that it might be the same ghostly vehicle seen in different places. The first is seen at the Molesworth Arms Hotel late at night. Unlike the other ghost coaches of Cornwall it is not driven by demons, nor does death follow in its wake. It is a simple, straightforward ghost. From descriptions by those who have seen it, this seems to be a typical stagecoach of the era immediately before the arrival of the railways. It is pulled by four stately horses and driven by a man wrapped up in a heavy coat and hat as if he were about to brave the winter cold. The coach materialises in the yard, moves at a walk out through the arch to the main street, then turns left and vanishes.

The Molesworth Arms was, in former days, one of the main coaching inns of Cornwall. Presumably the phantom coach is one of those that stopped here on its journeys along what

The old bridge at Wadebridge is crossed by a phantom coach late at night when cars are rare.

is now the A39 from Bristol to Penzance. Why it should return to haunt its old home nobody can tell.

The second ghost coach is seen, again only late at night, rattling over the ancient bridge that crosses the River Camel in the town centre. From its appearance it may be the same as the coach at the Molesworth Arms. Certainly the ghost at the inn turns as if heading downhill toward the bridge before it vanishes. Or it might be a quite different phantom that merely looks similar.

Some folklorists who have looked into the various stories about ghostly coaches in Cornwall and elsewhere have been struck by the fact that they are said to be seen very often on roads that lead inland from sheltered and remote bays and harbours. It has been suggested that these phantoms are, in reality, the vehicles used by smugglers to carry their contraband inland. Perhaps the smugglers spread the stories about ghostly coaches with demon drivers waiting to snatch away souls in order to terrify the locals. People who came across a coach moving at night were less likely to ask awkward questions about where it was going and what it carried if they thought that it might be a dangerous ghost.

The idea has attractions, but where it can be proved that smugglers have used such stories, it has always been that they were taking advantage of an already existing belief rather than making one up completely. The ghost coach at Lulworth in Dorset is a case in point. A coach really did overturn there in the 1740s and the ghost of the coachman was reported several times before the smugglers elaborated the tale for their own purposes. The best that can be said is that the ghost coaches of Cornwall have life – if that is the right word – all of their own that owes nothing to the nefarious activities of the smugglers.

GREY LADIES

Of all the ghosts that might be encountered in Britain, none is so numerous nor so elusive as the grey lady. Every county, almost every town, has its own grey lady haunting some lane, road or house. They are as ubiquitous a phantom as could be met anywhere.

Camborne, not to be outdone by any other Cornish town, has not merely got a grey lady. It has got three of them. The phantoms appear in Truthall Lane, where they stroll along quietly enough, dressed in the long, whitish gowns traditional for this type of phantom. One night, back in the 1890s, a mine captain was making his way home down Truthall Lane late one night when he met the three grey ladies coming the other way. He prudently stepped out of their path, but then his courage returned and he hailed them.

'Where be you bound, then?' he asked. The ladies moved on quietly for a few seconds, then they stopped. One of the ghosts turned to face the man, who was by now regretting his bravery.

'The living have naught to do with the dead,' the grey lady stated. Then she and her companions moved on to fade from sight.

The white lady of Godolphin House, a lovely Tudor mansion near Penzance, can be identified. She is the phantom of Margaret, Lady Godolphin, who died in 1678. She is said to appear on the anniversary of her funeral. The precise date of this has not been preserved, though her tomb in the nearby church records her death as having taken place on 9 September. It probably does not matter too much in any case. Her ghost has been seen moving through the house on various dates, though usually in the autumn.

The ghostly white lady seen around Luxulyan churchyard also has an identity. She is the wife of a vicar 'from way back', according to locals. Sadly nobody can quite recall her name. She is a gentle soul, it would appear. She glides about among the tombs, then fades quietly from sight. Equally peaceful is the white lady of St Levan. She frequents the churchyard on summer evenings and has been reported from time to time for at least the past two centuries. She does not seem to scare anyone, merely to startle people who had thought that they were alone in the tranquil churchyard. Not so the white lady of Ludgvan, who is anything but retiring. She is tall and wears a hood that covers her head and shades her face from view. She moves purposefully around the churchyard and, unlike most ghosts, has been known to follow people about. One man visiting the churchyard thought that the ghost was watching him as well as following him and became quite unnerved by the incident.

Also rather startling could be the grey lady of Marazion. These days she is less offensive than she was in days gone by. She is seen now as a rather lonely figure that stands beside the coast road overlooking Mount's Bay. Her gaze is baleful, but otherwise she is not particularly alarming. In the days before motorised transport, however, she was rather more frightening. This lady was in the habit of jumping up behind riders and digging her heels into the flanks of the horses. Urged on by the ghostly rider, the horse would bolt. The human rider would hang on for dear life, while the ghost laughed and shrieked her delight. Only when the ghost hopped off again could the steed be got under control. It is to be hoped that she never learns how to drive a car.

Bochym Manor, outside Mullion, has a ghostly lady who is unusual in two ways. First she appears in a pink dress, not one of grey or white. Second she is rather shorter than is usual, with one witness describing her as being only about 4ft tall, though others put her at 5ft. This lack of height has led some researchers to speculate that the Pink Lady of Bochym might in fact be a ghostly child.

However, the story attached to her would indicate that she was at least a mature teenager. The girl lived about 250 years ago and was a younger daughter of the family that then lived in the manor. Her lack of a good dowry, as well as her lack of height, meant that the girl was not considered to be a good catch in the marriage market. This may have put off the sons of local squires and landowners, but did not deter the teenage groom who looked after the horses at Bochym Manor. The two youngsters fell in love and planned to marry. The girl's

Luxulyan churchyard.

The white lady of Ludgvan haunts the area around the church.

father, however, would have none of it. There might not be a queue of young gentlemen forming to marry his daughter, but that did not mean that he wanted to have a horsegroom for a son-in-law. What happened next is not entirely clear. The groom left the district, though whether he was bribed, bullied or beaten into leaving was unknown. The girl clearly blamed her father and locked herself in her room for days. When she did emerge it was with a broken heart. She would not eat properly and soon pined away and died. After her death she returned in her favourite pink gown, which she had planned to wear at the wedding, to haunt the house.

Back in 1916 a naval officer stationed nearby happened to be walking past the gates to Bochym Manor one evening. The moonlight was bright and he could see his way clearly enough. He happened to glance toward the house and saw on the grass in front of the manor a most curious scene. Two men dressed in shirt sleeves and breeches were fighting with swords. Curious, the officer stopped to watch. The fight went on for some time, and the officer gradually began to feel uneasy. It began to dawn on him that what he was watching was not real in some way.

Suddenly one of the men thrust his blade deep into the chest of the other. The second man fell and lay prostrate and still on the turf. The first man bent down as if to check the man were dead. Then he turned and waved. A group of half a dozen men now appeared and began to walk toward the two duellists. At that point the surviving fighter looked up and seemed to see the naval officer. He pointed with his sword to the witness, as if drawing the attention of the approaching men to his presence. At this point the naval officer stepped backward, stumbled and fainted. When he came to, apparently only a few minutes later according to his watch, he was quite alone. There was no sign of the fighters or the other men. Had he seen a phantom duel, or a real one? Was the duel somehow linked to the Pink Lady? There are more questions than answers at Bochym Manor.

One of the finest stately homes of Cornwall is Lanhydrock House, just outside Bodmin. It was built in 1642 for Lord Robartes, just as the English Civil War was getting underway. It survived that upheaval, but in 1881 a fire broke out that spread rapidly through the building. Despite the best efforts of estate workers, most of the house was gutted. Starting in 1883, the house was rebuilt. The exterior walls of the damaged sections were left as they were, but the interior was completed as a state-of-the-art Victorian mansion with all the latest gadgets and facilities that the developing technology of the era had to offer. It has scarcely changed since and offers a magnificent window into the 19th-century past. The house is in the care of the National Trust.

There are two lady ghosts here. The first walks through the part of the house that escaped the fire of 1881. She is seen most often in the Gallery, though she has sometimes appeared in the Drawing Room. She wears a long black gown that reaches to the floor and is clearly rather elderly. She walks with a firm enough tread, however, as she wanders about the old house. This ghost is usually identified as being that of Lady Isabella, wife of the Lord John Robartes who was the son of the builder.

A different phantom lady has been seen in the rebuilt section of the house, usually in Her Ladyship's Room. This ghost is identified as being that of the Lady Robartes who was in residence at the time of the fire. She was aged 68 and was rescued by servants who manoeuvred her out of an upstairs window onto the shoulders of a burly gardener and so down a ladder. She never got over the shock and died a few days later.

Another fine mansion open to the public is Trerice House, near Newquay. This elegant manor was built in 1573 on an E-shaped plan by Sir John Arundell. Sir John had led an adventurous life. At the time the Protestant cities of the Netherlands were in open rebellion against the Catholic Spanish overlord. The rebellion attracted many idealistic young Protestants, such as Sir John, as well as the services of some hard-bitten mercenaries. This phase of Sir John's life left a clear mark at Trerice, for the gables of the house are curved and decorated with scrolls in the Dutch fashion.

The ghost of Trerice belongs to two centuries or so after Sir John's time. The Arundell of the time had a reputation among the locals as something of a wicked squire, with his heavy drinking, wild gambling and collection of equally wayward friends. Among his various escapades was the seduction of a servant girl who subsequently died in childbirth, or committed suicide depending on which version of the story one cares to believe. It is her ghost that haunts the North Wing of the house. She is said to glide along the Gallery or to walk down the stone staircase. Often she is accompanied by the scent of lavender, which may also manifest itself when the ghost is not seen. During the 1970s the North Wing underwent renovations and repairs. The work seems to have disturbed the grey lady, for she walked more often when the workmen were in than she did before, or has done since. It is rumoured that the Wicked Squire Arundell has also returned in spectral form, but no reliable witnesses of this ghost can be found.

Another fine Cornish house to be haunted is the old manor at Leedstown. The grey lady here, according to a local rhyme,

'Runs up and down the stair

And sits and weeps and sleeks her hair'

She is said to have been a young lady who inherited the house when still a teenager. Her property attracted a number of suitors, and she had the misfortune to fall in love with one who was as dishonest as he was handsome. As soon as the pair were married, he took out a huge mortgage on the property and fled to America with the cash to begin a new life abroad. The young lady was left with the debts and little prospect of marrying again. No wonder she weeps so disconsolately. The house is not open to the public.

In the spring of 1644, Royalist Cornwall had already driven off one invasion by Roundhead forces from further east, and a second invasion force was gathering in Somerset. This was, therefore, a very bad time for young Kate Penfound to tell her staunchly Royalist father and family that she had fallen in love with John Trebarfoot. The Trebarfoots were a good enough family, but they had known Parliamentarian sympathies and at least one of their number was off fighting with Cromwell somewhere. Unsurprisingly, Kate's father forbade the marriage and wrote to John Trebarfoot banning him from Penfound Manor. The young lovers were not to be denied, however. Young Trebarfoot made arrangements for an elopement and one evening, traditionally 26 April, he arrived at Penfound Manor. Kate was waiting for his signal and came hurrying down the stairs and into the courtyard.

Unfortunately her father had suspected something was planned, and was waiting for them with pistol and sword. He emerged from the shadows with his pistol pointed at young Trebarfoot. Kate sprang between the two men, and fell dead from the bullet that her father had aimed at her lover. Trebarfoot then attacked. The noise of gunfire had roused the house, and servants came running in time to see Trebarfoot fall with Squire Arthur Penfound's sword through his heart. The ghost of Kate Penfound has been seen many times at the house, both in the hall and her bedroom. She is dressed in a white gown, presumably her would-be wedding dress that she never wore. There have also been the sounds of ghostly footsteps and of doors opening and closing when nobody was present. In recent years the noises have been more frequent than the ghost.

The town of St Ives has two ghostly ladies, while a third lurks nearby. The most tragic haunts the shoreline. This is the ghost of a lady who was rescued from a shipwreck in the bay by local fishermen. She was dragged senseless from the storm-lashed waters. When the lady began to recover her sense, she asked for her baby. No baby had been rescued. Distraught the lady grabbed a lantern and raced down to the beach to search for her child. The waves claimed her and her body was found a few days later after the tempest had died down.

It is her ghost that is seen wandering the shoreline at dusk, holding aloft an old-fashioned lantern. She walks quickly, peering into the gloom as if searching for something. The locals believe that she appears only when bad weather is in the offing, though this does not always seem to be the case.

Another grey lady haunts Fore Street. This is the ghost of a wealthy old lady who lived in Knill's House. Whenever the lady went out she was in the habit of wearing the fine jewels that had been left to her by her husband. After her death in the 1850s her ghost began to be seen, dressed likewise in the magnificent jewels of which she had been so proud. The ghost was seen so often that the townsfolk would hurry past Knill's House, particularly after dark. In latter years she has been seen less often. Indeed, this particular ghost may walk no more, as no reliable sighting has been recorded since the 1950s.

Not far from St Ives once stood Consols Mine, with the particularly productive Wheal Mary Shaft. It was here that the Lady in Black used to be seen. She appeared most often near the Wheal Mary Shaft, but could appear anywhere about the mine workings. She appeared dressed all in black with a black hat and black muffler. The ghost was usually taken to be the widow or mother of a miner who had died down the pit, but nobody was really certain. In the 1890s a man named Noall came across the ghost unexpectedly as he walked around a corner. Recovering from his shock, the man admonished the ghost by saying 'Thee art a greet fool to stand there frightening honest people like thee dost, and never answering nothen when they do spake to thee.' The words were barely out of his mouth when the Lady in Black turned to look at him. A gust of wind blew his hat off his head. The miner turned round to pick the hat up, but it was nowhere in sight. Nor was the ghostly woman when he turned back to face her. Next day the hat reappeared. It was found lying close to the entrance to the Wheal Mary Shaft. It was torn to shreds.

HAUNTED PUBS AND HOTELS

Anyone familiar with Cornwall will know that its pubs, inns and hotels are among the most welcoming in Britain. The importance of the tourist trade to the Cornish economy no doubt has much to do with it. The publicans and hoteliers of Cornwall are used to catering for the needs and desires of travellers and holidaymakers, and have been for centuries. They must also be used to dealing with spectres and phantoms for a good number of the county's pubs are haunted.

One of these is the Tinners Arms at Zennor. Nobody has been able to identify this particular phantom, for he is never seen. There can be little doubt that he exists, however, for he is forever moving glasses about, hiding small objects and otherwise making a bit of a nuisance of himself. A barmaid who worked at the pub in 2007 was certain of his presence, saying that she had heard his footsteps moving about upstairs quite clearly when she was in the downstairs bar getting ready to open up, or clearing away after the pub had shut. The invisible ghost was not though of as being particularly unpleasant or scary, he was just part of the pub.

The small stone statue of a tin miner stands over the door to the haunted Tinners Arms at Zennor.

The Punch Bowl Inn in Lanreath harbours what might well be the most dangerous ghost in Cornwall.

Very different and altogether more sinister is the phantom that lurks at the Punch Bowl Inn in Lanreath. The ghost is now kept securely locked up, but in its day it was one of the most notorious and active spirits in the county. There are many here who still dread that it should ever get loose. The story began back in the 18th century when the vicar of Lanreath was an elderly widower of untidy habits but some personal wealth. He was, therefore, the ideal target for local matrons with daughters to be married off. In time the vicar chose one such young girl, who was admirably trained in domestic skills and could be counted on to keep a tidy house and minister to the sick. Then a handsome young curate arrived. Before long village gossip had it that the young wife and the young curate had taken to each other rather too warmly. The old vicar, it was said, was being betrayed under his own roof.

Gossip turned to deep suspicion when the vicar suddenly died. He had been dining with his wife and curate when he realised there was no wine to hand. The vicar headed for the cellar, but fell down the steep stone steps and broke his neck. Did he fall or was he pushed? The suspicions of the village were enough to drive the young widow back home, but the curate stayed on to minister to the parish until a new vicar arrived. He even officiated at the funeral of the man he was suspected of killing. The very day after the funeral, the trouble began.

A huge jet-black cockerel arrived in the village. Nobody knew where it had come from, and it was bigger than any cockerel anyone had even known. It was also downright evil. It hung about the churchyard and the vicarage. It would burst into raw-edged screeching whenever the curate came into view, puffing its feathers and flapping about in a fit of fury. If anyone approached the bird, they were driven back by a frantic onslaught of pecking beak

The ghost of Lanreath's Punch Bowl Inn is kept securely locked inside this oven.

and tearing claws, which drew blood and inflicted pain. Soon the bird grew bold enough to attack anyone it could reach. There could be little doubt, the villagers thought. This was the spirit of the murdered vicar come back to wreak his revenge.

Finally, the villagers had had enough. They gathered together with nets and sticks, determined to capture the cockerel. They cornered the bird against the churchyard wall and threw their nets. But the bird flapped into the air and escaped through the open window of the Punch Bowl Inn. It flew across the bar and into the oven by the fire. The quick-witted kitchen maid slammed the oven door shut and, locking it fast, trapped the irate bird. There it has remained ever since. No one dares open the oven door in case the vengeful spirit trapped within breaks loose and plagues the village once again.

Debbie, the landlady of the Punch Bowl in 2002, was asked if she had ever been tempted to open the oven to see what was inside.

'No!' she replied most firmly. 'Not after all that trouble we had last summer.' What trouble? 'Why, with the door in the corner there.' She pointed to a door in the corner of the main bar. 'It's meant to lead to a tunnel that descends down to the church vault. Some of the village lads wanted to explore the tunnel. They came over with torches one evening and I opened the door for them. They went down and found the tunnel went for some distance deeper and deeper, but was blocked by a fall. They said they would come back a few days later with shovels and props to clear the blockage and get further down the tunnel.'

Debbie stopped and eyed the door carefully.

'Then the trouble began. Stuff was moved around in here. You know, glasses and furniture and stuff. Then I was hoovering one day and the hoover just stopped. It had been switched off at the wall, but nobody else was in here. Then one of the staff heard voices even though the room was empty and locked at the time. I wasn't having that. I locked that door and blocked it up with that heavy wooden settle you see there now. Things quietened down after that. I'm not opening that door again, I can tell you. And I'm not taking chances with the oven either!'

The Ship Inn at Mousehole is another pub where the resident ghost seems to be quiet at the moment. It was, however, very active back in the 1960s and 1970s. The phantom took the form of a young man dressed in perfectly ordinary everyday clothes of the time. He was seen most often in the upstairs areas, and more than one witness thought that he was a solid human being – until he faded away, and vanished into thin air. Unlike some ghosts that disappear in an instant, this ghost faded away, becoming first transparent and then vanishing completely. He has never been identified. Penzance's Dolphin Inn has another inoffensive ghost in the form of a young man. He was killed here in an accident in 1873 and has returned to wander about the ground floor and cellar ever since.

Lostwithiel's Royal Oak pub has an equally retiring phantom. She is a rather attractive young lady dressed in a long green dress of finest silk. She seems to date from the 18th

Mousehole's Ship Inn was much haunted in the 1970s, but the ghost is now quiet.

Lostwithiel's Royal Oak pub is haunted by a rather gentle Lady in Green.

century judging by the fashions that she wears. According to a barmaid who worked at the pub in 2004, she does not bother anyone. 'She just sort of hangs about.'

Looe has more than one haunted pub, but the most haunted is the Buller's Arms close to the old fishing pier. The first is sensed near the back door of the pub. He often opens toilet doors and the back door, letting them bang shut. He was a bookies' runner in the days when off-course betting was illegal and often used to dodge in and out of the pub avoiding the authorities and the landlord, whose wife he was rumoured to be seducing. The second is a more playful spectre, who often stalks the bar, tapping shoulders on the way. He will also rearrange flowers, for which he appears to have a strange liking, and may move the beer or belongings of someone who does not do things the Cornish way, 'dreckly'.

The bar at the Buller's Arms is haunted by a bookies' runner from the days when off-course betting was illegal.

The staircase in Lostwithiel's Royal Oak pub where the Lady in Green is seen, most often walking upstairs.

Looe's Buller's Arms has no fewer than three ghosts.

He once threw a piece of cake from a freshly cut birthday cake across the room in front of many guests.

The third form of phantom activity is associated with the smuggling traditions of Looe. Muffled whispers can be heard late at night when the staff are clearing up the empty bar. These are thought to be the murmuring of phantom smugglers plotting their next enterprise. In the old days of the 'fair traders', as they called themselves, the Bullers Arms was something of a centre for these men. It was here that they would meet to arrange rendezvous points and prices for their contraband. The pub was favoured because it was so small that any strangers, who might be informants for the Revenue men, would have been easy to spot. If you tap the slates at the window end of the pool table you will hear the hollow echoes of a former tunnel used by the smugglers to gain access to the beach.

'They're no trouble, you know, our ghosts' reported a man who worked at the Buller's Arms in 2004. 'They're just playful like. Not frightening at all, just a little frustrating at times.'

The second haunted pub is on the other side of the harbour from the Buller's Arms. This is the appropriately named Jolly Sailor, without doubt a charming pub. On chill winter evenings a stove is kept burning to warm the place.

It seems that two centuries or more ago there was a pretty young farm girl living at Talland, a few miles west of Looe. The girl fell in love with a fisherman in the port of Looe and the romance blossomed quickly. He, however, did not truly return the girl's feelings but looked on his amorous conquest as little more than a bit of sport.

When the girl fell pregnant and demanded marriage, the fisherman just laughed at her. He had made no promises, he said, and if she had not been careful it was her own lookout. He returned to drinking with his pals in the Jolly Sailor. Needless to say the girl's family were not best pleased and came looking for the heartless fisherman. He had, however, left on a merchant ship bound for foreign ports. He returned from time to time, drinking with his friends in the Jolly Sailor and joking of his conquests of foreign girls. Each time he had gone before the girl's family could catch him.

Whether the poor girl from Talland killed herself, or died of a broken heart or a difficult birth, is unclear. But die she did, and from that moment on the heartless sailor's fortunes changed. Every time he put into Looe, he found himself plagued by a white hare. The malevolent creature would follow the man around, staring at him with blazing red eyes filled with hate and loathing. The sailor tried to catch the hare and kill it, but it always managed to evade him, disappearing in the dark corners when he thought he had it trapped. Then it would appear again and follow in his footsteps. Local people had no doubt what the white hare was. They had seen it running down from Talland whenever this man's ship put into port. It was the ghost of the wronged girl come to exact revenge.

Slowly the man's friends began to avoid him. They did not want to suffer the baleful stare of the phantom white hare, and he found it difficult to gain work on a ship – or even

The Jolly Sailor at Looe is haunted by a heartless rogue who came to a sticky end.

The Westcliff Hotel in Looe has a ghost that appears only when the haunted room is empty.

a local fishing boat. Nobody wanted to share whatever fate the vengeful spirit had in store for the man. Then one day he was found dead on the quayside. If the good folk of Looe thought they had seen the last of the white hare they were wrong. On moonlit evenings when the tide and wind were just right for merchantmen to put into port, the white hare would run down from Talland and scamper to the quayside in front of the Jolly Sailor. There it would watch the incoming ships until the last had tied up before capering around the square and running off back towards Talland.

The third of Looe's haunted hostelries is the Westcliff Hotel. When spoken to, Jill the manageress reported that 'There is a ghost of a man in the upstairs back room. You never see him, just hear him clumping about in big heavy boots, usually when the room is empty. You hear him from the room underneath. We don't let the room out much, but nothing to do with the ghost – who never bothers anyone when the room has got someone in it – just that it has no view of the harbour or sea so it is the last to be let when the hotel is full.'

The Jamaica Inn at Bolvenor, high on Bodmin Moor, is home to several spooks.

The haunted bedroom at the Jamaica Inn where the man in the tricorn hat appears.

Jamaica Inn at Bolvenor, high on Bodmin Moor, is famous as the setting for the classic novel by Daphne Du Maurier. It is also known for its ghost, or rather ghosts. Nobody is entirely certain how many there are lurking in this welcoming ancient inn.

Given its naval connections, it is not surprising that one of the ghosts at Jamaica Inn is a sailor. He sits on the stone wall outside the pub as if waiting for a coach or a friend to come along the main road from London to Penzance. If so, he waits in vain. The road outside the inn is no longer the main road, for a modern bypass takes the hurtling traffic a few hundred yards to the north. Which makes this a more peaceful place than it would otherwise be.

The sailor is, however, rarely seen. Far more active is the man in the tricorn hat, who haunts Room No. 5. This room is on the first floor in the oldest part of the inn. The room dates back to the 16th century, so a gentleman in 18th-century clothing would be quite at home. Glen, the general manager, said 'He appears over there by the window, usually in the small hours of the morning. Then he walks across to the cupboard and vanishes.' Does he do anything else? 'Not really. Well, he can muck about with clocks and watches. Last Thursday a lady staying in this room was late to breakfast because her alarm clock had stopped in the middle of the night. That would be the ghost. She didn't see him. But it was him. He likes stopping clocks.'

A different ghost is seen down in the main bar. 'See that table in the far corner, by the window? That's where the old man sits. He has grey hair and is dressed in dark, old-fashioned clothes, which are a bit shabby as if they are wearing out. He just sits there and stares out the window. We don't like him much. We had a psychic in here a little while ago. She said he was dishonest and shifty – a real crook.'

Val the cook was, in 2004, the longest-serving member of staff at the inn, having worked there nearly 30 years. Val said 'We sometimes see a smokey shape of a human at the far end of our restaurant. Can't make out if it be man or woman, but it drifts about like it is looking for summat. But the real ghost appears in that there doorway.' She pointed to the door that led to the car park. 'It be a man in a green jumper – yes modern like. Sort of thing people wear these days. I saw him one night when we kitchen staff was sitting here eating our meal after a big do. He just stood in the doorway watching us. Then he turned round and walked out to the car park. Gave me a real turn it did. I had locked that door shut just five minutes earlier. And it were still locked shut when we tested it. I tell you this is a good place to work. But it is odd. You never knows who is watching you. Never knows who is watching you. Very odd.'

There are other phantoms at Jamaica Inn. Some are seen rarely, others are only heard. Some put in an appearance once, then are not seen again. A few years ago the Ghost Club carried out an investigation here and reached the conclusion that the inn is a major centre for psychic energy. Perhaps this is because it stands at the centre of a whole network of ley

The ghosts of the Jamaica Inn are found in the older parts of the pub that cluster around the courtyard.

The Jamaica Inn's ghostly man in a green jumper is seen in this doorway.

lines, those ancient lines that link sites of sacred importance. A copy of the Ghost Club report is available from reception at the Jamaica Inn and it makes very interesting reading. Just what you need when taking a break to enjoy one of the tasty dishes on offer to hungry travellers, or to hungry ghosthunters.

The town of Helston has two haunted pubs, or rather it did. The first to house a ghost was the Market Place's Beehive Inn, now a trendy wine bar. He was a very active spectre in the 1970s, but faded in the 1990s and has not been seen since the place stopped being a pub. Dressed in a jumper and slacks, he was every inch the fashionable 1960s gent about town. He was seen walking in through the front door, but he never got so far as the bar. Nobody ever recognised him, so maybe he was the wraith of a tourist.

Almost opposite the former Beehive in the Market Place stands the Angel. This is still very much a pub, though a grand one with function rooms and restaurant. The bar area has been built out over what was formerly the coaching courtyard, which is why it has a 40ft deep well in it. The well has been topped by a sheet of strong glass to be used as a table, but it is still possible to peer down into its depths. There is an ancient priest hole in the bar, near the front window. This dates back to the days when the Angel was the town house of the Godolphin family. Whether they hid a priest in it might be doubtful as it is a bit on the small side. Perhaps it was used for valuables. It was discovered quite by chance when the floor was

The haunted ballroom of Helston's Angel Hotel has a minstrel's gallery dating to the days when this was home to Lord Godolphin.

being repaired. Today it has a wooden trapdoor lifted by a brass ring instead of the old hidden spring-loaded door of past years.

The ghosts of the Angel gather upstairs at the back of the pub in what was originally the Godolphin's Ballroom, then the Mayor's Banqueting Suite and is now the Angel's function room. It is a grand chamber with an orchestra balcony and impressive decor. It is this room that is haunted. The phantom may be that of Mrs Mary Ann Bennetts, the landlady from 1833 until her death in 1875.

The Kenegie Hotel, outside Penzance, is haunted by a woman in black. She is thought to be a housekeeper from the days when this was the private mansion of the Bolitho family. That family sold up in 1920, so she must date to before then and, judging by her dress, might be from the 1860s. She walks through the downstairs rooms in her long black dress with a bunch of keys dangling from her waist. The lady in black is not the only ghost at the Kenegie. There is also the phantom of a young woman in the kitchens. This ghost is never seen, but the merry sounds of her attractive laugh will often echo around the room when work is done for the day. A third spectre, or it might be one of the other two, is also never seen. It lightly brushes the cheeks of girls with an invisible hand.

The Manor House Inn at Rillamill underwent a rather spectacular haunting in the 1960s. The sounds of heavy footsteps were heard coming from upstairs on numerous occasions.

The Manor House Inn at Rillamill underwent a rather spectacular haunting in the 1960s.

The landlady, Mrs McCloy, became so accustomed to the noises that she stopped paying any attention. The phenomenon stopped as suddenly as it had started.

Truro has two haunted inns, though little is known about either phantom. The Star Inn is haunted by a young woman. The story goes that she was a servant seduced and murdered by an evil landlord of years gone by. If so, he covered his tracks well for no record of any such crime has ever been found. The William IV pub has a rather shadowy ghost that is rarely seen clearly. He seems to be wearing a cloak of some kind, and is for this reason usually said to be a ghostly monk.

CHURCHES AND CLERICAL GHOSTS

Given that generations of Cornishfolk have been buried in churches, it is hardly surprising that these places of worship and their surroundings are the haunt of ghosts and phantoms. Quite why clergymen should themselves seem to become spectres rather more often than more ordinary folk is not so clear. Perhaps their spiritual role predisposes them to return as phantoms.

The private chapel at Godolphin House is the haunt of a phantom funeral. The gloomy procession makes its way from the house along the tree-lined path to the chapel on summer evenings. Who is being buried and why the funeral returns so frequently is unknown. Equally obscure was the origin of the spirit which, in 1761, came to the church at Ludgvan. This ghost was seen flying through the air, then attacked one of the pinnacles, which came crashing to the ground. The villagers of Ludgvan were adamant that the ghost was that of a man from Treassow, though how they knew this is unclear. Rather more sinister, though thankfully rarely encountered, is the gruesome phantom that lurks at Launceston churchyard. Locals describe it as a kergrim, a type of spectre that feasts on the flesh of the dead.

The ghost that haunts the church of St Ladoca at Ladock is far more active, being encountered on numerous occasions. The ghost is described as being that of an elderly man in rather old-fashioned clothes of some dark colour. He certainly wears a jacket and a hat. His usual trick is to enter the church when a person is in there alone. He will be seen to open and close the door, then walk off as if to sit in a pew, but then he vanishes utterly without leaving a trace. He will also enter when the bell-ringers are practising. He is widely believed to the phantom of a churchwarden and bell-ringer who died in the 1930s. It is presumed that he loves his church so much that he returns to ensure that it is properly cared for and that the bell-ringing is up to his exacting standards. Another former bell-ringer to return in spectral form is Captain Martin of Penryn. He was drowned when his schooner went down, but was quickly back as a ghost. He has often been seen in or around the church when the bells are being rung.

The small village of Little Petherick stands on the A389 between Wadebridge and Padstow. Where the road takes a sharp right-hand bend, a ghostly monk has been seen. He has never been noticed to do anything, but simply stands there watching the cars go past. The ghostly monk that haunts the old abbey church at St Germans is just as shy and retiring. He has been seen numerous times, but does little other than potter about near the church. Presumably he was a monk here back in the pre-Reformation days when this was an abbey. Before the Norman conquest of 1066, St Germans was the cathedral church of the Bishop of Cornwall. The Normans tore down the small stone structure that they found and erected the massive church that is to be seen today.

Another very old haunting is the ghostly vicar of St Neot's Church at Poundstock. This ghost has been flitting about the church and its churchyard since the 14th century. In the 1350s Cornwall was suffering the after effects of the Black Death. That dreadful plague had carried off about a third of the population in the space of two months, and returned every now and then to kill a few more. The sudden lack of people led to extensive social upheavals. Instead of there being a lack of good land, which gave landowners an advantage, there was now a lack of tenants and workers. This gave the edge in negotiations over leases and wages to the farmhands and farmers themselves. Rents fell dramatically. Even more disruptive was the fact that many serfs, who in theory were tied to their land by lifelong bonds of service, simply walked off and left. Landowners desperate for labourers to work their lands were offering cash wages to freemen, and many serfs preferred to give up their smallholdings and

The ghostly vicar of St Neot's Church at Poundstock has been haunting the churchyard where he was murdered for six centuries.

work for cash. This led to endless disputes between landowners and between landowners and workers. In theory these disputes had to be settled in the courts of justice, but so many men and women were on the move and conditions were so chaotic that it is hardly surprising that some preferred to settle their disputes by brute force.

It was against this background of chaos, upheaval and disruption that the vicar of Poundstock, William Penfound, began a remarkable series of sermons. The Penfounds were a wealthy family of landowners in this area of Cornwall, so it might be thought that William would have taken their side. Instead he preached for calm and tolerance for the claims of all. From his pulpit he asked that all men should lay down their weapons and seek a way forward through God's grace that would produce a just settlement for all.

Among those unwilling to listen to this message were John Bevill and Simon de St Gennys, a pair of varlets in the pay of local landowners. On 27 December 1356 they burst into the church while William was preaching a sermon. They ordered him to fall silent. When he did not, they dragged him out into the churchyard and stabbed him to death. The parishioners pounced on the killers and bound them hand and foot. The men were taken off for trial, but although they were convicted they were pardoned soon afterward. It is no wonder that the ghost of the unfortunate William Penfound should wander around his peaceful hillside church and the churchyard where he died. He would no doubt be relieved to learn that the violence against which he preached died down soon afterward, though it would be a generation before the economic aftermath of the Black Death was sorted out. It is possible to argue that we are still living in the post-plague world. Our economy is based on cash, not on land or on service.

The churchyard at Perranzabuloe is the venue for an odd ghost story from Victorian times. Apparently an old lady walking through the church yard one winter's day saw a pair of false teeth lying on the ground among the graves. Thinking she might find a use for them, she picked them up and took them home. That night she was woken from her sleep by an invisible hand banging on her window and voice calling out 'Give me back my teeth. Give me back my teeth.' The woman was terrified, but eventually summoned up the courage to open the window and fling the teeth out into her backyard. The sounds of footsteps heading off back to the churchyard were then heard. Next day she went out into the backyard. The teeth were gone and there was no sign of any human footprints to be seen. The town of Wadebridge stands on the River Camel, but a small tributary called the Hay flows in from the south. It is on the banks of the Hay that three monks have been seen.

The church at Stratton contains a most unusual and rather unnerving tomb. This is the grave of Sir Ralph de Blanchminster. The effigy that lies on top of the tomb is clearly enough that of a knight of the early 14th century, with chainmail and early pieces of plate. But the head is faceless. The heroic but unfortunate Sir Ralph had a sad life story. He was already approaching middle age when news reached England that the last Christian fortress in the Holy Land had fallen to the Moslem hordes. The fall of the city of Acre in 1291 sent shockwaves through Europe. Everyone had known that the crusaders were hemmed in and under pressure, but nobody seriously believed that the mighty fortress city would actually fall. Fall it did and many gallant knights rushed out to Rhodes or to Constantinople to join the front line between Christendom and an increasingly militant Islam.

Sir Ralph from Stratton was one of those to go. He was away so long, without sending word home, that his family and friends gave him up for dead. His wife, thinking herself a widow, remarried. Then the ageing Sir Ralph came riding home, some 20 years after he had left. He brought back no wealth except honour and the scars of war. Realising that his sudden arrival was going to cause problems for those he had left behind, Sir Ralph gave up worldly goods and took the vows of a hermit. So he lived his final years in holy solitude at Stratton. After his death, his ghost began to lurk around the churchyard. It is seen there still.

St Mary's churchyard in Penzance is haunted by a ghost that resulted from a practical joke gone badly wrong. Back in the 1830s, a certain Captain Carhew would dress up as a ghost to frighten people. He thought it very funny to leap out from behind tombstones making weird and unearthly noises. His neighbours were not too impressed at being regularly startled.

Then one day a sailor came ashore from a ship not knowing anything of Carhew and his pranks. As the sailor walked through the churchyard, Carhew sprang out at him. Unperturbed, the sailor demanded 'Who are you?'

Carhew replied 'I am one of the dead come back to haunt the world.'

'Then get back below under ground', growled the sailor and punched Carhew so hard that he fell unconscious. The unfortunate Carhew never really recovered. Soon after his death his phantom was seen returning to the place that he had once 'haunted' in jest.

UNTIMELY DEATHS

Sudden death seems often to leave its spectral mark on the place where it happened. Whether this is due to the high emotions of those involved, the brutality of the act or the reactions of the local people is unclear. But several of the ghosts in Cornwall have their origin in a sudden death.

One of the more complex of the murder and ghost legends of Cornwall centres on the Penrose family, who built the manor of that name near Sennen. Back in the 1680s the wife of Sir Ralph Penrose died. The heartbroken Sir Ralph decided to go abroad with his young son to try to forget the tragedy. Together with a cousin, William, he booked passage to the Americas with a ship out of Penzance. Sir Ralph left his home and estates in the care of his younger brother John.

The ship put to sea, but soon ran into trouble in the Western Approaches as a storm came sweeping in from the Atlantic. The ship was driven back toward Land's End. The captain, desperate to avoid being caught on a lee shore, managed to clear St Ives Head heading north-east, but the ship could not make it around Godrevy Point and was driven on to the Cowloe Rock. The survivors scrambled to take to boats and rafts while the storm lashed around them. Watching all this from the clifftops was brother John. He watched the ship founder, but took no steps to get help. He saw first one boat, then another swamped by the waves and did nothing. Then he saw a few bedraggled survivors crawling ashore. At last he took action. Racing down to the beach, John found his brother's body, then spotted the young son crawling up from the pounding surf. Snatching up a convenient rock John battered the boy to death, then carried the body out of sight of the fishermen who were now streaming on to the beach to look for survivors and any booty that might be worth picking up.

Having hidden his nephew's corpse, John hurried back to Penrose. He acted surprised when news was brought to him that his brother's ship had been wrecked. If John hoped to secure ownership of his ill-gotten house and estate quickly he was to be disappointed. Because the body of the boy could not be found the ownership of the estate was not clear. Although it was known that the boy had been on board, and that he was not among the survivors, it took some years of legal work to get him declared dead. Then John truly became owner of Penrose and all it contained. He married well and settled down to enjoy his wealth.

Unknown to the wicked John, his cousin William had survived the wreck. Washed ashore some miles away, he had completely lost his memory. Having been nursed back to physical health he became an itinerant farm labourer, having no particular skill. For some years he worked his way around Cornwall, always managing to earn enough to survive.

Then, one day, he came to Sennen looking for work. As he walked along the beach he was accosted by the ghost of his long-dead relative.

'My uncle did murder me,' the phantom boy said. 'I lie beneath the dead tree in the orchard. Dig to find me. Then dig to bury me.'

The shock caused William's memory to come flooding back. He hurried off to find Penrose servants who would remember him. Together they hurried to the orchard and began digging under the old, dead tree. They soon found the boy's skeleton and the smashed nature of his skull showed that the ghost had been speaking the truth. Rousing the magistrates, the now angry men marched up to Penrose to demand that John be punished.

Seeing them coming and realising that his horrible crimes had been unearthed, John hanged himself in a stable. The property then passed to William, but he could not bring himself to live there and the house was rented out for the rest of his lifetime.

Another family murder that became both a haunting and a legend happened at Bohelland Farm, near Penryn, in September 1618. A man was born into a poor family that lived at

Bohelland Farm. His sister married well, to a prosperous fisherman of Penryn. With her settled the man decided go to sea to seek his fortune, leaving what money he had to his parents so that they could continue to work the farm.

The long years rolled by. The young man travelled to the far Indies where he had many adventures, escaped death only narrowly more than once and finally made his fortune. Some 25 years after he left, the man returned to England and made his way to Newlyn. He called on his sister first, and learned that his aged parents were still alive. They had, however, given up farming. They rented out their lands to other farmers and ran Bohelland Farm as a guest house for those visiting the area. The returning son then had what he considered to be a great idea. He decided to go up to his parents and take a room, pretending to be a stranger lately returned from the Indies. Then he would see how long it took them to recognise him. The sister was not sure this was a good idea, but the man insisted. Quickly repacking his bags, he hurried off up the hill to put his plan into action.

After a couple of days the sister began to wonder how events were unfolding at Bohelland Farm. She had heard nothing and wondered if her parents had still not recognised their son. By the third day, she decided it was time the prank came to an end and walked up to Bohelland Farm. She found her father and asked after the 'traveller returned from the Indies'. Her father told her that no such man had called.

Puzzled, the woman told her parents of the traveller's true identity, then returned to Newlyn and organised a search party in case her brother had missed his way. Not long afterward a member of the search party called at Bohelland Farm to check that the brother had not passed by or moved on. He made a gruesome discovery. The mother was dead, bludgeoned to death, while the body of the father swung gently from a beam in the stables. There was a suicide note. In this the man confessed that when the man they took to be a rich stranger had arrived, he and his wife had given him a room. At dinner the man had shown them his purse full of gold coins and another filled with jewels, and had boasted of his much greater wealth in a bank in Plymouth.

The stranger had gone out of his way to tell the ageing couple that he knew nobody in or near Penryn. No doubt this was part of his prank, but it sealed his doom. After he had gone to bed the worse for drink, the mother had urged the father to kill the rich traveller and steal his cash and jewels. After much discussion, the father had given in to his wife's promptings. He had crept upstairs to murder his own son, whom he took to be a stranger. When he had heard from his daughter what he had done, the man had decided to kill first his wife and then himself. The suicide note ended with instructions on how to find the body of the murdered son. When she heard the news the murdered man's sister herself committed suicide, blaming herself for not having stopped the prank before it went so horribly wrong.

The story of this gruesome killing was spread by a pamphlet entitled 'News from Penrin in Cornwall of a most bloody and unexampled murder very lately committed.' That pamphlet was, some years later, taken up by the playwright George Lillo. He turned it into a melodramatic play entitled *Guilt its own Punishment; or Fatal Curiosity*, which was first staged at the Haymarket in 1736. This melodrama proved to be hugely popular. It was revived for decades after and was translated into German.

The details of the crime grew more and more lurid with each retelling. In 1814, the writers Daniel and Samuel Lysons decided to investigate the murder. They found that a man had been killed in the circumstances recorded, but could find no record of the sister having committed suicide. In their day Bohelland Farm was only a ruin, though locals knew where it had stood on the road to Roskrow. Apparently the house had been abandoned some 50 years after the murder due to the ghost that walked there. Even today the area can be disturbed by odd noises at night, and a few people have reported seeing a ghostly man walking purposefully up from Penryn towards Trevithal. Whether this is the ghost of the killer or the victim is not clear.

Cotehele is one of the grandest houses and estates in Cornwall. This fine stately home was begun in 1485 by Sir Richard Edgcumbe using the money that he gained by supporting the uprising that put Henry VII on the throne and resulted in the death of Sir Henry Bodrugan, referred to above. The house has scarcely altered since the 1650s when the Edgcumbes, whose wealth had continued to increase, built a new and much grander home at Mount Edgcumbe. Sir Richard's original clock of 1490, for instance, remains. It has no face, but has two bells to ring out the time.

The house has a number of ghosts. The oldest of these dates back to before the present house was built. During the reign of the Yorkist King Richard III, Sir Richard Edgcumbe was in secret correspondence with the Lancastrian claimant Henry Tudor, later Henry VII, who was then living in France. As the spring of 1485 turned to summer, the plans of Henry Tudor developed quickly. Sir Richard Edgcumbe was given the task of raising men for the Tudor cause and stopping the Yorkist forces from Cornwall marching to join Richard III. A messenger from Henry came to Cotehele to discuss the final details with Sir Richard. The two were overhead in their plotting by the ferryman who worked the nearby ferry over the Tamar. Not only was the man's ferry an important crossing for any armed force, but he was a known Yorkist sympathiser. Realising that he was listening to treason being plotted, the man fled. Sir Richard gave chase. The pursuit ended on the little bridge that crossed the stream that flows into the Tamar just south of Cotehele. Sir Richard cut down the hapless man.

Thereafter the ghost of the murdered man was frequently to be seen pacing back and forth over the bridge, while the stone on which he had died had an indelible bloodstain that no amount of scrubbing could remove. The bridge has since been rebuilt and the bloodstain has gone, but the murdered man's ghost remains to continue his supernatural pacing.

A second ghost is linked not so much to a death as to an almost-death. In about 1710 the then Lady Edgcumbe fell dangerously sick of a fever. For days she hovered between life

The haunted bridge at Cotehele is the second structure on the site.

and death, before finally giving up all signs of life. Her grieving family arranged a suitable funeral and laid her to rest in the family crypt beneath the floor of the church at St Dominick.

The night after the funeral the sexton, a dishonest fellow who had noticed a fine gold ring being buried on the finger of the dead woman, crept down into the vault. He prized the lid off the coffin and began to struggle with the ring, trying to pull it off the finger. Lady Edgcumbe suddenly sprang back to life, causing the sexton to flee screaming. Recovering her senses, Lady Edgcumbe then picked up the sexton's abandoned lantern. Still in something of a daze, she walked back to Cotehele and knocked on the door. The servant who answered collapsed in a faint, but soon enough Lady Edgcumbe was escorted to her chamber. Food and warm drink restored her gradually to health and a year later she gave birth to a baby boy who grew up to become the first member of the family to enter the House of Lords, as Baron Edgcumbe in 1748.

It is presumed that the lady who haunts Cotehele is this Lady Edgcumbe, though there does not seem to be any firm evidence linking the two. The ghost is dressed in a flowing gown and has long hair. She is usually described as carrying something, one witness thought that it was a bunch of flowers. This spectral lady is usually blamed for the scent of freshly cut herbs and the phantom music that sometimes fills the air in the old part of the house.

In 1813 an apparent murder came to light when an old inn on Penzance Quay was demolished to make way for a tin warehouse. Hidden underneath the floor in the private quarters was found the skeleton of a man. Locals soon began to talk of a sailor who had vanished in around 1780 after coming ashore from a ship. At the time not much attention had been paid to the man: he was just one penniless sailor who had slipped away rather than pay his bills. However, once the skeleton had been discovered rumours began to circulate that he had been carrying a fair sum of money that belonged to his employers. Inevitably, perhaps, it was said that he had been murdered by the inn keeper for the money. Who the skeleton really belonged to, how it had got there and how long it had lain hidden nobody ever discovered. What was quickly apparent was that digging up the bones had disturbed the spirit of whoever had been buried there. Although the skeleton was given a decent burial, the ghost continued to be seen hanging around the quay late at night. He is seen still, from time to time.

It was an accidental death that led to the haunting of the stableyard at Trerice House, near Newquay. One day in the early 19th century something frightened the carriage horses as they were being led into harness. They bolted, knocking down and killing a stableboy as they did so. His ghost has been seen several times walking around the stableyard, now the home of the souvenir shop and restaurant.

Just as fatal was the case of mistaken identity that took place in Chapel Street, Penzance, in 1880. A Mrs Baines had a house there with an apple tree in the garden. The apple tree had great sentimental value, having been planted by her long-dead husband, so Mrs Baines took great exception when the apples began going missing over night. She set her manservant, John, to guard the tree. Late at night, Mrs Baines went out into the garden to check up on John and was most angry to find him snoozing quietly. Greatly annoyed, she decided to pick some apples herself and take them to the kitchen, then return and wake up John to accuse him of allowing the apples to be taken while he slept. Mrs Baines accordingly plucked some apples and began to carry them to the house.

John woke up at that moment. Seeing a dark figure moving silently toward the open kitchen door, he leapt to the assumption that it was a burglar and, still groggy from sleep, blasted off with his shotgun. Mrs Baines fell dead. Her ghost began to walk in the little garden, around her precious apple tree, almost at once. She appeared as she had done in life, with her old-fashioned lace cap, laced sleeves and a gold-headed cane. In 1890 she was reported as being seen in her old house. The haunting continued for some years before the phantom Mrs Baines moved out into Chapel Street itself. She is still seen from time to time.

Another fatal accident led to the haunting of Wheal Jowell Mine. A miner fell to his death from a ladder. His ghost was later seen in the mine on several occasions. The dead man had had the habit of climbing ladders with his candle stuck into a ball of clay and held in the thumb and forefinger of his right hand – he used the remaining three fingers to hold on to the ladder. On more than one occasion his disembodied hand was seen holding a candle in this distinctive fashion.

The ghost of Porthgwidden Beach is, so far as those who see it are concerned, a white horse that trots along the shoreline. Locals have it that the spectral horse is the ghostly mount of a Mr Birch who was drowned here when swimming in the 19th century. The horse waited for his return and kept breaking loose to return here. Nobody could get the horse away, so it was left on the beach for days until it vanished. It waits still in ghostly form.

Near Wendion the ghost of a suicide victim named Tucker haunts the three-way crossroads outside the village. The unfortunate man was buried here since the unforgiving 19th century forbade a suicide to be buried in the churchyard. Another suicide haunted the Polbrean Mine at St Agnes for many years. Anne Corcas killed herself by leaping down the main shaft, though the reason for her action was never discovered. Her voice was later heard calling to miners from dark places to distract them from their work. One miner responded to the calls and the mine roof fell in where he had been working. Answering the ghost had saved his life.

At Altarnum, legend and literature have got hopelessly intertwined. In Daphne Du Maurier's book *Jamaica Inn*, the villain of the piece turns out to be the vicar at Altarnum. This fictional vicar runs a murderous smuggling gang, using his clergyman's house and travels as a cover for the illegal business. Locals may now tell you that the picturesque little bridge that leads to the church is haunted by a malevolent vicar. Whether the book copied the legend or the legend grew out of the book is unclear. In any case, the ghost of the wicked clergyman has not been seen of late.

ASSORTED GHOSTS

There are in Cornwall a number of ghosts that do not fit into any particular category. This may be because they are somewhat enigmatic in themselves, or that the details of the haunting have not be properly recorded – it must be admitted that a number of owners of haunted properties prefer not to court publicity and, as a result, the details of the spectre can be difficult to collect. Even when the details are to hand it is sometimes necessary to keep certain facts hidden at the request of the either the property owner or the person who encountered the ghost. Nevertheless these phantoms are all part of the mystery of Cornwall.

One of the most famous of these phantoms is that of John Tregeagle, which is reported from various sites around the county. John Tregeagle was steward to John, 2nd Lord Robartes of Lanhydrock House, and died in 1655. As a qualified lawyer, Tregeagle was much in demand to draw up legal documents of various kinds, as well as being a keeper of financial accounts.

It gradually became clear, however, that Tregeagle was a wicked and a greedy man. He would slip innocuous-seeming clauses into contracts and agreements that would later turn out to be of great advantage to himself. Accounts that he prepared were not always what they seemed. Sums of money, sometimes of a significant size, would somehow slip away from the accounts and into Tregeagle's pocket. He was, nevertheless, a charming and credible swindler who managed to continue to inveigle people into his clutches. He married a rich heiress and, after she died, an equally wealthy widow.

After his death numerous stories began to circulate about him. It was said that he had murdered his first wife for her money and to free himself to marry the second. His grave in St Breock's churchyard was said to be empty as Tregeagle had sold his soul to the Devil. It was also said that Tregeagle's family had been forced to pay a huge sum to have him buried in consecrated ground, and that even then the vicar of St Breock refused to have a memorial erected to such a notoriously wicked man. There is, indeed, no memorial to him to be seen. Such tales pale into insignificance compared to what is said to have happened five years after his death in the Assizes courthouse at Bodmin.

A case had come to trial between two landowners who were in dispute over a loan. The arrangement had been made through Tregeagle, but the contract that he had drawn up was so convoluted and complex that only he could really understand it. Since he was now dead, the two landowners were disagreeing over exactly how much interest should be paid and when it was due.

When the case came to court, the judge read through the document and, whether he fully understood it or not, announced a settlement. The man who asked to repay the money protested that he was being asked to pay too much too quickly, then finished by saying 'And I wish to God that Tregeagle were here to come and declare it.' Barely were the words out of his mouth than the ghost of Tregeagle stalked into the court. Before the astonished eyes of all present, Tregeagle's phantom bowed low to the judge, then rounded on the man who had summoned him. 'Pay what is due,' snapped the spectre. 'Thou has found it easy to bring me from my grave. But thou wilt not find it so easy to put me away.' Then he turned and strode from the court.

Sure enough, it was soon obvious that the ghost was not going to go away quietly. He began pestering those who had annoyed him in life, and particularly dogged the footsteps of the man who had been rash enough as to summon him from the grave. After some weeks those being plagued called in a number of local vicars and parsons, begging them to lay the ghost and rid them of his nuisance. At a most sombre ceremony the assembled clergymen cast their rituals of exorcism, but they found Tregeagle too powerful for them. They could not return him to the grave, nor even get him to leave Cornwall. Instead they could merely give him a task to do. After a quick consultation they decided to ask him to empty Dozmary Pool on Bodmin Moor using nothing but a limpet shell.

Given the size of Dozmary Pool, this task promised to take the spectral Tregeagle a very long time. The fact that the pool is replenished by an underwater spring faster than he could

The phantom of the infamous John Tregeagle, the wickedest man in Cornwall, haunts the shores of Dozmary Pool on Bodmin Moor.

empty it seemed to ensure that the task would take forever. Thus, it was hoped, Tregeagle was effectively laid to rest. It was not to be. Tregeagle was nothing if not wily. He somehow persuaded a minion of Hell to come to Dozmary Pool and take over his task. Soon Tregeagle's phantom was back to its tricks.

More exorcists were called. This time Tregeagle was given the task of weaving a rope of sand on Gwenvor Cove, then carrying it up to the rocky pinnacle of Carn Olva. This time the task seemed to be working. Years passed and there was no sign of Tregeagle's ghost. Then there came a winter with an exceptionally hard frost – the world was then going through one of its periodic cooler periods, known as a mini ice age. Tregeagle took advantage of the cold to scoop water out of Vellandreath Brook to soak the sand. As the fresh water froze, the sand became solid, allowing Tregeagle to complete his task. Freed from his supposedly endless penance, the ghost was let loose again to work evil through all Cornwall. The exorcists were called a third time. This time they summoned up St Petroc first to ask his advice. The holy man told them to set the wily Tregeagle a whole series of impossible tasks.

This they did. First he had to weave ropes of sand to stretch from Padstow to Rock. Then he had to clear Bareppa Cove of sand, carrying it all to Porthleven. Then he had to carry all the sand from Porthcurnor Cove to Nanjizal. When he had finished that he was to rebuild the ruined St Michael's Chapel at Roche using nothing but sand. Even though he was bound to all these tasks, Tregeagle had not yet finished causing trouble for the good folk of Cornwall. By dropping sand as he carried it, he managed to build up the sandbar that runs from Bareppa Cove to Porthleven, forming a navigational hazard for seamen.

When storms rage over the county he breaks free completely to go raging and roaring over the moors and uplands. Some say that you can hear his howling in the wind at Castle-an-Dinas. Others are sure that he prefers to frequent Tregagle's Hole, a natural stone arch near Carne Beacon.

There can be no doubt that the vast majority of stories told about Tregeagle are folklore or exaggeration rather than the truth. At this distance in time it is impossible to tell just how wicked John Tregeagle actually was. During his lifetime he was never convicted of any crime, though there were a few rumours. The main accusations against him were made after he died, and they rapidly snowballed to portray him as a sort of ultimately dishonest lawyer and educated scoundrel. Perhaps he was the wickedest man in Cornwall, or perhaps his reputation was invented by those who held a grudge. It is just one more mystery that Cornwall hides.

Then there is the haunted farmhouse located somewhere near Bossiney. The haunting was included in the works of an authoritative paranormal investigator, but the actual site was kept secret at the wishes of the owner. The haunting was well attested and is typical of many of the less famous ghosts of Cornwall. The farmhouse was, and probably still is, haunted by the ghost of an elderly man with stooped shoulders. He is seen sitting at an upstairs bedroom window staring out toward the distant sea. On occasion he may move an object in the room if he takes a disliking to it, or to its location. Generally, however, he is inoffensive and quite passive. Presumably he is waiting for some ship to come in. Who he was in life and why he haunts the house are quite unknown.

Camborne has an impressive number of these enigmatic ghosts, three in fact. The first is the phantom mine captain. He kept an office in the town where he used to sit close to the doorway buying and selling shares in the various local tin mines. He died in the 1880s and for the next 50 years or so his spectre was seen often sitting in the doorway as if watching passers-by for a familiar face. He has not been seen since World War Two, and neither has the second of Camborne's ghosts. This was a rather more gruesome apparition, being that of six men carrying a coffin that was seen heading toward the churchyard on moonlit nights. One woman who saw this ghostly group in the 1890s refused ever again to go out on moonlit nights, a habit she maintained until her death some 30 years later. The third ghost is the only one to be reported in recent years. This is the man in black who haunts the appropriately named Deadman's Cove a short distance along the coast. He appears to be looking out to sea, but vanishes if ever anyone approaches.

The Bedruthan Steps is a dramatic and famous stretch of coastline that is favoured by holidaymakers for its startling beauty. It is also much frequented by the lifeboats that are called out to rescue walkers cut off among the rocks by the tide. It is neither walkers nor seamen that haunt this scenic spot, but tin miners. There used to be a tin mine here in the 18th century. The ghostly indistinct shapes of men have been seen emerging from the ground where the mine shaft used to be. The sounds of the tap-tap-tapping of the miners' hammers has also been heard on still, quiet days.

Jew's Lane near Godolphin Cross is said to be haunted by a spectral bull pulling a blazing chariot. According to an old folklore book, this is the ghost of a Jew who hanged himself from a tree in the road and was buried at its foot. This is one of those ghosts of which many people have heard, in which some people believe, but that nobody has actually seen. It is likely that this particular phantom has rather more to do with folklore than an actual haunting.

The bull and blazing chariot are symbols of mithraism, a cult religion that in later Roman times came to be one of the main rivals of Christianity for official recognition. Mithras was in origin a Persian sun god, but his worship spread west at around the time of Christ and by AD100 was firmly established in Britain. He is always shown killing a bull, as the sacrifice of a celestial bull, in Mithraic belief, ensured the fertility of the Earth. All mithraic temples were built underground, either in caves or cellars, and the ceremonies were carried out in near darkness. The blazing chariot symbolised the role of Mithras as the Sun. The religion of Mithras was open only to men, who alone could take part in the underground ceremonies. As a result it became particularly popular with soldiers in the Roman army, and it seems that it was they who first brought the religion to Britain. By around 300 the cult was on the wane and by 400 had been overtaken by its rival, Christianity.

It may be that the story of the spectral bull and blazing chariot might indicate that there was a mithraic temple somewhere in this area. The story of the hanged Jew may indicate that some non-Christian person either committed suicide or was killed here. It is not beyond the realms of possibility that some dramatic event occurred at the time when Imperial agents were closing down pagan temples and forcibly transferring their wealth and property to Christian churches. Perhaps a priest of Mithras refused to hand over his temple's golden regalia and was summarily executed here. Whatever the truth, an archaeological survey of the area might prove rewarding.

Another apparent suicide haunts the B3297 as it climbs up out of Helston to head toward Wendron. What is now a roundabout was formerly a crossroads and so a suitable place for the burial of a suicide, consecrated ground being forbidden to them. The name of the unfortunate suicide was remembered only as Tucker, but he had a very active ghost. He was very often seen standing close to his burial place. More than once the phantom would step forward if a coach or cart passed by, as if trying to hitch a lift. Needless to say, nobody ever stopped for him.

A ghostly farm wagon is said to trundle along the road that leads from St Ives to St Ives Head. The coachman's whip may be heard to crack as he wields it with expert skill, but the horses' hooves make no sound at all as they strike the road surface. The old horse trough that used to stand in Ludgvan was, apparently, haunted by a woman who was seen washing her clothes in a basin beside it from time to time.

In the 1950s the Cornish press was filled with stories of 'The Haunted Chest of Morwenstow'. The wooden chest in question had been acquired second-hand and brought to Stanbury Manor, near Morwenstow, by the owner, Mr T. Ley. The chest had come from a house sale in Newlyn. As the story was later put together by the local press, the events had unfolded something like this.

In about 1890 a Newlyn man died leaving as his joint heirs his two daughters. Among the assorted bric-a-brac, antiques and accumulated debris of a long life, the girls found an old wooden trunk that they could never remember having been opened. It was locked shut. They called in a local expert in such matters who was of the opinion that the trunk was probably Spanish and could be as much as 300 years old. The two young women quickly dubbed it the Armada Chest and speculated that it had been taken off one of the ships that formed the Spanish Armada sent to invade England in 1588.

Some time later one of the girls found a key. Together with her sister she tried it on the Armada Chest and was delighted when it turned. They opened up the chest. What they saw was so horrible that they were both struck instantly deaf. They locked the trunk, refusing ever to reveal what they had seen nor to allow anyone else to open the Armada Chest. It was from the house of these two, by then very elderly, deaf sisters that Mr Ley had acquired the trunk. He was, at first, unaware of its history. The trunk was a fine piece of furniture, but without a key he could not open it. He put it temporarily in the armoury, and that evening six old guns fell off the wall. It was then moved to a bedroom to await the arrival of a locksmith to open it up. That evening a painting fell off the bedroom wall. Next day two more came down. In each case neither the hook nor the wire was broken or damaged in any way.

When the chest was eventually opened by a locksmith, it proved to be completely empty. Things continued to fall off walls in its vicinity, and it was this that got the chest into the press. The press stories prompted letters from people in Newlyn recounting the story of the deaf sisters. As the months passed the disturbances at Stanbury Manor faded and then ended.

Looe Island is said to be haunted by a ghostly man who has noticeably long, elegant hands. A skeleton matching the description was found in the 1890s, but there were no indications as to who he was, nor to how long the bones had lain there. What must be one of the most unnerving ghosts in Cornwall is to be found on Lodge Hill on the southern outskirts of Liskeard. It appears only after dark and only to people alone and on foot. Nobody in a car or walking in a group has reported the phantom, which makes it all the more creepy. Narrow lanes crowded in by overhanging tree branches can be spooky enough by moonlight, but they are 10 times worse when a ghost is about.

'I remember it from when I was a schoolgirl,' a Liskeard lady named Jackie reported. 'We all knew about it back then. I had to walk down Lodge Hill on my way home from school. It was fine in the summer as it was daylight when I made the journey, but winter was another matter. Especially if I had stayed behind for music lessons or, um, detention. Not that that was very often. Anyway, then I had to walk down the hill in the dark. And that was not funny at all.

'You see, many years ago a woman was drowned down the bottom of the hill. A frightful thing it was too. All sorts of splashing about and screaming involved when she drowned. And then her ghost came back to haunt the road. You'd be walking along minding your own business when suddenly there'd be this ear piercing scream and the sound of splashing. Frighten you out of your wits, it would. I used to run down that hill I can tell you. No dawdling about for me.'

Interestingly this road is now designated the B3254, running from Liskeard down towards Looe. But north of Liskeard the same B3254 is the haunt of a lane dog named Carrier. It seems to be a rather more supernatural road than most.

The victims of a drowning in the stream that flows through Lamorna are rather less terrifying. Just above the village there used to be a watermill, which had a deep pool into which the water fell as it tumbled over the watermill. It was here that two children were drowned. Exactly how they met their deaths is unknown as they were playing out of sight

Lodge Hill, on the southern outskirts of Liskeard, is haunted by a most disturbing phantom.

of home at the time. Their ghosts are seen playing quietly and picking flowers along the banks of the stream, just north of the village toward Trewoofe.

The town of Padstow has long been a favourite with holidaymakers, though more recently the TV celebrity chef Rick Stein has made it something of a mecca for fine food enthusiasts. It is now busier than ever, especially in the summer months. The oldest building in the town is the part stone, part-tilehung Abbey House that overlooks the harbour on its seaward side. The house is certainly mediaeval, but nobody is quite sure exactly how old it is. There seem to be two ghosts here. The older of the two is a young woman of Tudor days. She is seen walking up the staircase and is sometimes heard muttering to herself. Those who have seen her describe her as appearing to be very sad or melancholy. The second ghost appears at the first floor gallery window, peering out over the harbour. She is usually said to be an older woman, but no detailed descriptions are available. She is seen only for a fleeting moment, then is gone.

Genvor Cove near Land's End is said to be haunted by a band of raiders – some say Spanish, others Vikings – who landed here in the hope of obtaining plunder and pillage. Instead they met a band of armed local men who fought them back to the beach where a heavy swell was running. Those who escaped the Cornishmen were drowned in the surf. It is the ghosts of these raiders who are said to be the shadowy figures seen moving about the cove.

Pentillie Castle fell into ruin in the mid-20th century and most of it was demolished. This must have displeased the phantom of a former owner, even though it is not known to have been seen at the castle itself. The ghost in question is that of Sir James Tillie, a famous eccentric and conspicuously generous host, who lived here in the later 17th and early 18th centuries. Although Sir James was rumoured to be an atheist, he proclaimed himself fully confident that he would rise again two years after his death and return to live once more at Pentillie Castle.

When Sir James Tillie died in 1712 it was found that his will left detailed instructions as to a most peculiar burial, and the funds to pay for it. He insisted that he was to be buried on top of Mount Ararat, a hill just north of the castle. To be buried voluntarily outside of consecrated ground was shocking enough in that age, but Sir James went further. He was to be dressed in his very finest clothes, complete with hat and wig, then seated upright in a chair. On a table beside him were to be set a bottle of wine and a glass, with which to refresh himself when he came back to life, plus papers proving his ownership of Pentillie Castle so that he could prove his right to live there. Everything was done as he wished. Two years later, on the day that Sir James was due to come back to life, drink his wine and stroll home to Pentillie Castle, not much happened. In the days that followed, not much continued to happen on a regular basis. But then stories began to circulate. The locals said that they had seen Sir James, or rather his ghost. The phantom was seen walking down from Mount Ararat towards Pentillie Castle. The spectral squire never seems to have got back to his former home, however. Today his ghost haunts the hill and the lane that runs down it.

Another famed eccentric haunts the streets of St Hilary. This is the 18th-century cleric the Revd John Penneck. When alive, Penneck led an exemplary life. He was a respected scholar and worked his way up through the church and lay hierarchy to become Chancellor of Exeter. He haunts his old home village, which seems reasonable enough. What is not clear is why the phantom should be in such a towering rage. Those who see him report that he stamps about waving his fists in the air as if raging. What the matter might be we do not know for his performance takes place in absolute silence.

The isolated pinnacle of rock at Roche is topped by a ruined chapel that was probably built in the 15th century. A shadowy figure has been seen moving about the ruins, but nobody has ever got a clear enough look to be able to identify the phantom. Some think that he — it is probably male — is a miner. Others that he is a monk or maybe a leper. Nobody knows. Nor is anyone certain who or what it is that haunts Bridle Lane at Talland. Some people say it is smugglers, others that it is demons, while some believe both tales are mere inventions produced by smugglers keen to keep law-abiding folk away from the area at night.

The cliffs around Polperro are riddled by caves, one of which is haunted. This time we do at least know the identity of the hapless man whose phantom is to be met here. His name was Willy Willock, a local fisherman. One day back in the early 19th century young Willy announced that he was going to explore the caves of Chapel Hill for no better reason than in the hope of finding out what was in there. Willy's fellow villagers tried to dissuade him, but he was determined. So one morning bold Willy set off into the caves armed with only a lantern. A couple of his friends sat down outside the cave entrance to await his return. The minutes turned to hours. Then the friends heard the welcome sounds of Willy's footsteps coming back toward the mouth of the cave. They called out to him, and heard Willy calling back. Then Willy's voice and footsteps faded away again. When they next heard him approaching the friends were getting worried. It was coming on to dusk by this time and surely Willy's lantern would be running low on oil? They shouted and called to young Willy Willock. They heard him shout back that he was coming out, but again his voice and footsteps receded into the distance. This time Willy was heard of no more. His friends waited loyally all that night and into the next day, but there was no sign of him. Nobody felt brave enough to go down into the cave, so the mystery was never solved. Willy's ghost returns to Chapel Hill from time to time. His voice has been heard plaintively calling out from the caves asking for directions back to the surface, but poor Willy is beyond all human help.

So are the phantoms that hover about Comprigney Field just outside Truro. This is the place, just outside the city walls, where the execution gibbet formerly stood. It is haunted, they say, by the spirits of those who ended their lives here. They are, unsurprisingly, mournful phantoms.

EXORCISTS, ETC.

If Cornwall had more than its fair share of ghosts, phantoms and spectres, it also had a large number of clergymen who were skilled and practised in the arts of exorcism – or 'ghost-laying' as the process was known in Cornwall. A local gentleman writing in 1826 stated 'I could mention the names of several parsons whose influence over their flock was solely attributable to this circumstance.'

Among the best known of these was the Revd Jago of Wendron. It was said that no spirit on earth could withstand his powers. He was called in to deal with supernatural troubles of all kinds from one end of Cornwall to the other. It was said that he never took a groom with him because he had harnessed one of the ghosts that he had vanquished to perform this task for him. When he arrived he would let his reins drop to the ground, then turn and lash the reins with his whip. It was widely believed that this called up a phantom to hold the reins. More likely he had perfected the art of 'ground tieing', meaning that a horse will not move from a spot once its reins are laid on the ground.

Parson Woods of Ladock habitually carried with him a stout ebony walking stick on which were engraved mystical figures and astrological signs. With this he would lash out when conducting an exorcism, apparently landing heavy blows on the spirits and demons that remained invisible to those watching the ritual. It was a performance that never failed to impress. The Revd Richard Dodge of Talland was famous not only among his flock, but among his fellow clergy. He took up his post in 1713 and held the parish until his death. In the 1740s Parson Mills of Lanreath wrote to Dodge, and the letter has been preserved:

My dear brother Dodge

I have ventured to trouble you at the earnest request of my parishioners with a matter, of which some particulars have doubtless reached you and which has caused and is causing much terror in my neighbourhood. For its fuller explication, I will be so tedious as to recount to you the whole of this strange story as it has reached my ears, for as yet I have not satisfied my eyes of its truth. It has been told me by men of honest and good report with such strong assurances that it behoves us to look more closely into the matter.

There is in the neighbourhood of this village a barren bit of moor which had no owner, or rather more than one, for the lords of the adjoining manors debated its ownership between themselves and both determined to take it from the poor, who have for many years past regarded it as a common. And truly, it is little to the credit of these gentlemen that they should strive for a thing so worthless as scarce to bear the cost of law, and yet of no mean value to the poor labouring people. The two litigants, however, contested it with as much violence as if it had been a field of great price, and especially one an old man had so set his heart on the success of his suit that the loss of it a few years back is said to have much hastened his death. Nor indeed, after death, if current reports are worthy of credit, does he quit his claim to it. For at night-time his apparition is seen on the moor, to the great terror of the neighbouring villagers. A public path leads by at no great distance from the spot and on divers occasions has the labourer, returning from his work, been frightened nigh unto lunacy by sight and sounds of a very dreadful character. The appearance is said to be that of a man habited in black, driving a carriage drawn by headless horses.

This is, I avow, very marvellous to believe but it has had so much credible testimony and has gained so many believers in my parish that some steps seem necessary to allay the excitement it causes. I have been applied to for this purpose, and my present business is to ask your assistance in this matter, either to reassure the minds of the country people if it be only a simple terror; or if there be truth in it to set the troubled spirit of the man at rest.

My messenger, who is an industrious and trustworthy man will give you more information if it be needed for, from reports, he is acquainted with most of the circumstances and will bring back your advice and promise of assistance.

Not doubting of your help herein, I do, with my very hearty commendation, commit you to God's protection and blessing and am

Your very loving brother

Abraham Mills.

The moor in question was the area around Blackadon, which stands about two miles south of Lanreath. By the time Mills sent his note the ghost had been seen by at least eight people, probably more, and heard clattering past their barricaded windows by several more. Dodge sent a note, which has sadly not survived, back to Mills stating that he was busy the following day visiting the sick of his parish, but would ride over the following day. This he did, arriving at Lanreath in the early afternoon. The two clergymen debated what to do. They decided that, as the evening promised to be fine, they would ride up to Blackadon Moor at dusk to await the arrival of the ghostly coach. They accordingly went up and waited on the lonely moor, passing the time discussing scripture and the affairs of their parishes.

By 3am nothing had happened, so the two clergymen decided to call it a night and go home. Mills headed off for Lanreath while Dodge headed for Talland. He was riding up out of the steep little valley that lies between Hendra and Polean Farm and approaching a group of prehistoric burial tumuli when his horse suddenly shied. Dodge could see nothing wrong, so he put his spurs to the horse. Again it refused to go on, this time skittering backwards as if frightened of something. Dodge dismounted and began leading the horse forward. The steed took a few steps, then stopped again and went back on its haunches. Clearly it was determined not to go forward. Accepting the situation, Dodge remounted and headed back toward Lanreath. He passed over the haunted moor safely enough, but as he began the ride down to the village Dodge saw something large and black blocking the road ahead of him.

As Dodge trotted towards the obstruction, his horse again stopped suddenly and refused to go on. This time Dodge dismounted and continued on foot. To his horror he saw that the black object was the much discussed phantom coach pulled by ghostly horses. Even worse was the fact that lying on the road with the ghostly coachman bending over him was the prostrate body of Parson Mills.

Dodge fell to his knees and began to pray with all the fervour that he could muster. Within seconds the stomping hooves fell silent. Dodge continued to pray, though he felt a most malevolent evil spreading over the place. Then a hollow, haunting voice boomed out.

'Dodge is come. I must be gone!' There then followed the sounds of horses moving off and the rumbling of coach wheels.

When silence returned again, Dodge looked up. The phantom coach had gone. He hurried over to Mills, and was relieved to find that he was still alive. Mills came to and was clearly in some distress. He blurted out that he had met the ghostly coach, that his horse had bolted and that he had fallen to the ground. The last thing he remembered was seeing the awful spectral carriage bearing down on him. Dodge then saw lanterns and torches approaching from the direction of Lanreath. Mills's horse had bolted home and its arrival had awoken his servant. That man had then woken up others in the village. Notwithstanding their terror of the ghostly coach they had gathered in a bunch, armed themselves with whatever weapons lay to hand and were now marching to try to find their parson and rescue him from whatever threatened. They were relieved to find Dodge and Mills unharmed. Mills was carried back home and, after a few days of bed rest, was fully recovered. The dramatic events quickly found their way into the local newspapers and into magazines in London and abroad.

There can be little doubt that the main outlines of this amazing story are true. They appeared in print while both Mills and Dodge were still alive. It is unlikely that any publisher would have risked printing the story if it were not believed to be true and frankly incredible that neither clergyman would have complained. What should be made of this event is unclear. Some people choose to view it as proof of the superstitious nonsense that was believed by uneducated rural folk in the 18th century. Others think that there must be more to it than that. It may well be that a ghostly coach did indeed haunt the lonely moor as described. Others, however, think that the tale may have been related to smuggling.

The haunted spot was on a quiet lane from Looe to Bodmin that avoided the main roads, but which was fully passable by coach or cart. Looe is known to have been a smuggling port, and Bodmin was a known transshipment centre for the illegal trade. Leaving aside the supposed paranormal aspects of the story, the events could have a perfectly human explanation. Smugglers not infrequently took advantage of stories about ghosts, witches and the like to spread fear among the law-abiding folk and so ensure that they stayed indoors when the smugglers were at their work. The ghost coach was said to frequent the moor, but it was heard also clattering through villages and past isolated cottages. This would seem to be more like a smuggler's cart than a ghost coach.

It may be that Mills came across this smuggler's cart, all decorated up to appear more ghostly, as he left the moor. His horse may have bolted and he was thrown, only to faint as the supposed phantom approached. When Dodge arrived, he saw the coachman bending over Mills. A smuggler would surely have done just this to see if the clergyman was badly injured. The coachman's words 'Dodge is come. I must be gone.' would be perfectly natural for a smuggler. He would know that Mills would be in good hands and that he himself had best be off before Dodge recognised him for what he was.

This single and most famous event apart, Dodge continued to perform exorcisms and ghost-laying ceremonies throughout his long ministry. His preferred option was to send the unquiet spirits to the Red Sea to await the final call of Doomsday.

Parson Richards of Camborne was another noted exorcist. One night two tin miners were walking home and passed by the churchyard. They saw Parson Richards standing in the church porch with a Bible in one hand and a candle in the other while a horsewhip was hanging over his shoulder. He was reading aloud from the Bible. The curiosity of the miners got the better of them, so they walked across the churchyard to Parson Richards and asked him what he was up to.

'Ye damned fools,' exploded the clergyman in a sudden rage. 'What did ye want for to go breaking the spell like that. Two minutes more and I should have had that un fast in Hell. Now no one knows when I shall catch un again.' With that he seized the whip from off his shoulders and lashed at the hapless miners. The miners fled, with the vicar chasing them all the way home, plying his whip with great vigour.

Parson Polkinghorne of St Ives had a similarly robust reputation. His greatest feat was the calming of the ghost of Wild Harris of Karnegie. The clergyman's rites would seem to be fading in their power, for the galloping horseman has been seen again of late near to the ruined ramparts of Castle-an-Dinas. If even the powers of the famed Polkinghorne are fading, it is to be wondered just how many of the ghosts laid by famous parsons of old are about to rise again.

Cornwall has ghosts in plenty already. It seems as if it will soon have many more.

CHAPTER 8

MYSTERIOUS WITCHES

There has probably been more misunderstanding on the subject of witches than any other aspect of the mysterious across not only Cornwall, but also the whole of England. The truth is not, however, difficult to find for those who approach the subject with an open mind. Sadly, an open mind is exactly what most people do not have on this subject.

From about the early 16th century the more educated classes came to believe that witches were in league with the Devil. It was this that led to the widespread persecutions of witches that resulted in the deaths of hundreds of people across Europe. English law took a rather more pragmatic view of matters. The Witchcraft Act of 1542 did not make witchcraft itself illegal, but imposed punishments for injuries inflicted using witchcraft. A witch who used her magic to kill a person was to be hanged, for instance, while one who caused cattle to die was fined a sum of money. The peak of witchcraft trials in England came in the 1640s. The dramatic rise in cases was probably prompted as much by the religious upheavals of the time as anything else. Witches did not suddenly become more numerous, but the authorities were more willing to prosecute them. The spate of trials ended in the 1660s. The Witchcraft Act was repealed in 1736. It was replaced by a new law that made it illegal to take money or goods from people under the pretence of being able to perform magic.

From the 19th century on, the opinions of educated folk swerved rapidly in the other direction. Witches were no longer seen as agents of the Devil, but as harmless old women viciously persecuted by superstitious neighbours. This grew out of the rationalist belief that magical powers do not exist and so, by extension, witches could not exist. It followed therefore that any accused witch must have been innocent and a victim. In the 1950s a new strand of thought about witches began to appear that gained pace in the 1960s and 1970s. This began with the writings of Gerald Gardner, a British colonial rubber planter and customs officer who retired to England after World War Two. Gardner had long had an interest in the occult and in folklore – he was a member of the Council of the highly respectable and academic British Folklore Society.

In the 1950s Gardner produced a series of books on witchcraft. He claimed to have made contact with a group of witches in the New Forest who had inherited the traditions and rites of the ancient, pagan religion of the British isles by way of mediaeval witches. He claimed it was a religion that had long been an organised, clandestine religion in rural areas, but which by the 20th century was dying out. According to Gardner the rites involved a great deal of nudity and sexual activity. The religion of Wicca that he described was devoted to a veneration of the natural world through ritual and occult activity. Gardner's writings spawned the creation of a number of covens of newly converted witches, mostly in the English-speaking world but also in France. Most took as their main text the *Book of Shadows*, which Gardner claimed was the book given to him by the New Forest witches. It has since been shown that much of the *Book of Shadows* was based on earlier works about witchcraft, magic and third world religions. Despite this the Wicca faith, mixed with a deal of environmentalism and earth-mother theory, has continued to grow and may now count 100,000 adherents worldwide.

The most notorious witch of Cornwall was Madgy Figgy, who lived at Tol Pedn near Penwith at some indeterminate date. She was said to have consorted with a coven of witches at St Levan in her youth but in later years to have operated alone. She is said to have been a master of the black arts, but to have specialised in second sight – that is, the business of prediction.

On certain stormy days she would climb up to a stone formation above Porth Loe and sit down on a natural rocky seat, now known as Madgy Figgy's Chair. From there she would gaze out to sea. If she began to rub her hands and cackle with glee, the locals knew that a wreck was imminent. It was never entirely clear whether Madgy Figgy was merely foreseeing the disaster, or if she was causing it with her magic. Either way, a wreck inevitably followed her glee. The locals would gather on the cliffs to await the wreck. They were always careful never to go down to start searching the shore for valuables until Madgy Figgy had first taken everything she wanted. Only then could the ordinary people move in.

One day a foreign ship – some say she was Portuguese – came ashore after Madgy Figgy had been sitting in her fatal chair. Among the debris thrown ashore was the body of a young, beautiful woman wearing a fabulous collection of jewels. As soon as she saw the body, Madgy Figgy stopped short and glared. She summoned a group of local men, ordering them to carefully remove the jewels without damaging them in any way. The jewels were put into a stout box and the woman's body buried on top of the cliffs. Madgy Figgy stood over the grave in silence for some time, then gazed out over the stormy seas. 'It takes one to know one' she declared, then stalked off home. That night the awestruck locals saw a strange, eerie blue light emerge from the grave of the beautiful stranger. The light drifted over the hills to Madgy Figgy's Chair and hovered there a while before moving on to alight on the roof of the witch's house. Every night for three months the weird blue light was seen. Nobody dared ask Madgy Figgy what was going on. The old witch did not seem too bothered.

Then there came to Porth Loe a dark stranger who spoke not a word of English, but who paid for his lodgings and meals in good gold coins. Although he had never been seen before, the stranger seemed to know where he was going. One evening he walked up the hill to the spot where the beautiful stranger lay buried. He stood on the clifftop as if waiting. When the eerie blue light appeared, the stranger watched it carefully then followed it to first to Madgy Figgy's Chair and then down to her cottage. As he approached, Madgy Figgy appeared in the doorway. The two gazed wordlessly at each other for long minutes. Then Madgy Figgy nodded and went back inside. A few moments later she was back with the small wooden box containing the jewels in her hands. Without a word she handed them over. The stranger nodded, then turned and left.

Another witch, or perhaps wizard, of great power once lived at Pengersick Castle. The castle was built in the 14th century by Lord Pengersick. His wife died young and he married again with rather undue haste. This new wife was charming and beautiful, but she had a wicked heart and was, moreover, a witch. When she had a son, she decided to get rid of her husband's son by his first wife so that her own son would become the new heir. When Lord Pengersick was away from home for some weeks she sent him messages telling him that his eldest son was ill, then later that he had died. In fact she had sold him to Barbary Corsairs, who were always on the look out for white slaves to sell in the bazaars of North Africa.

The years passed. Lord Pengersick died and his second son inherited the castle and estates. One day he abruptly left, telling nobody where he was bound. The boy's mother, the witch, threw out her servants and lived alone. She was rumoured to have murdered her husband with magic and to be slowly turning into a serpent. Then the original heir came home to Pengersick. He brought with him a beautiful Saracen wife, and a considerable skill in the black arts. Hearing that his stepmother was alone in Pengersick Castle, the young Lord Pengersick just laughed. He strode down to the castle. Minutes later the witch was seen fleeing the castle to throw herself into the sea.

Then began dark days for Pengersick and nearby villages. The new Lord Pengersick soon showed himself to be a mighty magician. He never went to church and, when the vicar called on him one day, threw him out of the castle, kicking him down the road. He would ride out at night mounted on a great black charger. Galloping the lanes and fields, Lord Pengersick whipped anybody who got in his way. The beautiful Saracen lady did not mix in local society. She would sit down by the shore singing a most beautiful and haunting song in her own language. Mermaids, sprites and fairies would come to listen to her.

For years the Lord and Lady Pengersick lived their strange lives. Then a swarthy man dressed like a Saracen came to Marazion. Each evening he would walk out of the inn where he stayed, returning at dawn. One bold soul followed him. The stranger walked to the entrance to Pengersick valley, then sat on a stone where he spent the night gazing down toward the castle. Lord Pengersick no longer rode out at night. His wife no longer sang.

One evening the stranger did not stop at his usual stone, but walked on through Pengersick village toward the castle. Within minutes the castle was ablaze. Flames towered up into the sky. As the locals gathered, they saw three human figures flying and whirling around in the flames and smoke. Then there was a terrific explosion as if lightning had shot up from the blaze. The figures vanished. No signs of Lord or Lady Pengersick were ever found, nor of the stranger. The castle was left a hollow, blackened ruin.

The castle has now been restored and is a private house. The story outlined above is only one version of the story of the magician Lord Pengersick. There are many tales and legends about him, though all seem to agree that he married a Saracen lady and died in a fire. The tales may have been inspired by Lord Henry Pengersick, who lived here in the 14th century. Henry Pengersick was a follower of the religious reformer John Wycliffe.

Wycliffe translated the Bible into English for the first time and argued that the forgiveness of sins was a matter between an individual and God. This undermined the Church's teachings on confession and penance, from which it gained much wealth, and earned Wycliffe the enmity of the Church. He went on to condemn the Church for being so obsessed with earthly power and wealth, arguing that the Church had no right to enforce taxation in the form of tithes. After his death he was convicted of heresy and his bones were dug up and destroyed. Lord Pengersick took the teachings very seriously. He particularly agreed with Wycliffe's stand on tithes. When the tithe collector came to Pengersick Castle he was rewarded with a punch on the nose.

Such are the legends of witches of long ago. What of the facts? There have been witches in Cornwall for years. They have often been called pellars, both men and women going by this name. It is in tales of these pellars or wise women or cunning men that the truth behind the witches of legend can be found.

Most of these pellars were local people who had learned the arts and skills of using herbs and plants for medicinal purposes. Most pellars could produce a potion, poultice or rub to cure sore throats, rheumatism and other ailments. To preserve the mystery of their skill and to stop others learning their secrets, these pellars often dressed up their skills as being due to magic. Some seem to have practised hypnotism to enhance their reputations. Others made quite outlandish claims. It is beyond doubt that the powers of these pellars were firmly believed in by their neighbours, and therein lay much of their real power. Modern medical researchers know all about the so-called 'placebo effect'. This is the fact that some people will recover from a disease when they believe that they have been given a powerful drug, even when they have not. Some of the medical success claimed by pellars was probably due to the placebo effect.

The power of belief in witches' power went further than that. Some claimed the power to locate lost objects and to identify thieves. If an object was stolen, the local pellar might be called in. He would declare that the object would be found next day, and let it be known that if it were not he would use his powers to identify the thief and punish him by occult means. Because the thief did believe that the pellar had the power to do this, he would return the stolen item.

A well-documented incident of this kind occurred in the 1850s. A man who lived on Lady Downs had a purse of money stolen from his house when he was out working. He went to see the local pellar, who said that he would cast spells for the return of the money.

The pellar then went walking to all the local villages recounting what had happened and declaring that he was collecting the ingredients for a very powerful spell that would bring calamity on the thief. The spell would be cast, he said, the next day. That night the purse was returned.

Many pellars did not actually charge for their services, and those that did asked only for pennies. They worked mostly for people who did not have much money and so could not afford high fees. Instead the witch gained payment by way of respect in the local community and by acts of kindness. Nobody wanted the local pellar to go without food or clothing. Farmers would offer part of their crops to the pellar, and wives would take round nicely cooked meals or spare items of clothing.

There was, however, a darker side to the life of the witch or pellar. Some chose to use their undoubted influence and very real powers to persecute those people they did not like. A farmer might be told that all his cattle would die unless he gave one animal to the witch. A herbal brew slipped into the cattle's water would ensure that they fell ill. When the desired gift was handed over the cattle would recover. The witch could be a figure of very definite power within a local community, able to instill fear as well as hope. It is perhaps no wonder that if an individual pellar went too far then the community would seek retribution. Only when modern medicine was able to explain and cure diseases of both animals and humans did the hold of the witch on rural communities begin to diminish.

The scale of the power and influence of the witches in Cornwall can be gathered from looking at a few true cases from the 19th century. One of the most famous and powerful of these figures was Tamson Blight of Helston, often referred to as Tammy the Pellar, who died in the 1870s. One woman who consulted Tamson Blight was suffering from paralysed legs so that she could not walk a step. The sickness had come on quite suddenly. Unable to get to Blight's house on foot, the woman asked the vicar to take her in his pony and trap. The vicar, not unnaturally for a Christian minister, refused, saying that he 'did not believe in all such rubbish'. He eventually agreed to do so to placate the lady.

When she was consulted, Blight told the woman that she had been 'ill-wished' by a neighbour. The curse would be lifted only when the woman knew who it was that was wishing her ill. Blight said that the woman had to go home, then sit in her kitchen with the door open. Sooner or later somebody would come by and ask if anyone had seen her pet cat. That person would be the ill-wisher and the spell would be broken. The disapproving vicar got the woman back to her cottage and settled her in the kitchen chair. Just as the vicar was preparing to leave a neighbour put her head round the door to ask 'Has anyone seen my little cat?'. At once the paralysed woman sprang to her feet and hopped around the room completely cured.

Tamson Blight had other powers. Her husband was the chief engineer at a tin mine. One day when Tamson was at the mine collecting half-burned cinders for use on her home fire,

Tamson Blight, seen here in a contemporary portrait, was one of the most powerful witches of 19th-century Cornwall.

the owner came out to chase her off. Some valuable timber had been stolen from the minehead and he wanted nobody around who was not an employee. Tamson went and sat a short distance off, glaring at the mine. The steam engine that pumped water out of the mine stopped dead. Realising that he had offended the witch, the mine owner went to see her and invited her to return to her task. Tamson grinned. The engine restarted.

Another famous pellar was Uncle Jack Hooper of Redruth. He professed to have the second sight. He had an old mirror, covered in soot from his pipe. Hooper would stare into this to get the answers to the riddles that people brought him. Two particular instances were recorded by a local gentleman, Jim Thomas.

A woman went to see Hooper seeking news about her husband, a miner who had taken a job with a mine in Spain. Hooper opened the door, stared at her in silence for a moment then said 'I do know well enough what you have come for. You do want for me to tell 'ee something about your husband.' Duly impressed, the woman followed Hooper to his consulting room where he stared at his dark mirror for a few moments before declaring 'He's aboard ship on the high seas. I can see him now in this 'ere bit of glass. He is just starting up the rigging.' The man arrived home a few days later.

He was equally successful at solving a series of petty thefts from a farm. The items that had gone missing were tools that were not particularly expensive, but which caused much trouble by not being present when they were needed. Hooper advised the farmer to go home and find a toad. He was then to gather all his family and servants together in the kitchen, without telling them why they were there. The farmer then had to throw the toad on the kitchen fire and watch it burn. The next person to walk through the kitchen door would be the culprit.

The farmer did exactly as Hooper advised. While the hapless toad burned, the farmer turned to look at his servants, expecting one of them to make some excuse to leave the room. Instead, the door opened and in stepped the farmer's brother-in-law.

'What are you doing here?' demanded the farmer.

'Why,' the man replied. 'I just came to tell you that I have seen your cattle straying down the road as the gate has been left open.'

Needless to say the brother-in-law was accused of leaving the gate open and banned from the farm. The thefts stopped immediately.

Hooper did not always get things right. When a farmer called to consult Hooper about a sick cow he was led through to the consulting room. Hooper spent some time staring into the smoked mirror, then said 'Ah, 'tis plain enough to see here. Thee hast gone and lost a shirt down the mine and you want me to tell 'ee who has stolen it.'

In October 1892 a witchcraft case came before the magistrates at Liskeard. Elderly Elizabeth Wellington was well known as a pellar, but a woman named Harriet King became convinced that Wellington had ill-wished her, though the curse had for some reason fallen on her cat rather than on herself. One day King happened to meet Wellington and her daughter in the street. King accused Wellington of being a witch, using her powers for evil and denounced her loud enough for everyone in the street to hear. Wellington's daughter promptly launched herself at King, raining blows on her and scratching her face. She was convicted of assault and fined one shilling. 'The magistrates expressed surprise at the cause of the assault' the official record stated.

Another court case in 1887 touched on the belief that one way to neutralise a spell was to draw blood from the witch who had cast it. The children of a Cambourne woman named Pengerret fell ill with a fever just a few days after she had had a minor altercation with the local pellar. Believing that the witch had put a curse on her children as a result, Mrs Pengerret stormed round to see her. Mrs Pengerret pushed her way into the house and accused the pellar of casting a curse, then demanded that she lift it.

'I have not ill-wished your children,' declared the pellar. 'I do not go about with fever in my pocket.'

Mrs Pengerret was not to be put off. 'Then I must see your blood,' she screamed and scratched the pellar's face until it bled. Mrs Pengerret was hauled off to court and fined for her trouble, but the fever left her children next day.

This power to ill-wish was not always deliberate. In the summer of 1889 a fisherman at St Ives encountered a run of bad luck. All his fellows hauled in good, profitable catches, but he enjoyed only patchy luck. Some days he did well, other days he could not catch a thing. Puzzled, the fisherman consulted the local pellar. The pellar spent some time with the fisherman discussing what had happened and it transpired that the bad fishing trips always happened when the fisherman met a certain woman on his way to his boat.

'Leave 'un to me', said the pellar.

Next day the woman came to the fisherman and apologised for having caused him any trouble, but assured him that she had not intended any ill to the fisherman. She begged his pardon, which the fisherman gave. After that his luck changed and he was as successful as his fellows.

John Stevens of Polperro, who was active in the 1840s, used the stars as his guide. When he was consulted, he would turn to a wooden box in which he kept three brass plates engraved with the constellations and positions of the stars and planets. He would then manipulate the plates so that they moved over each other for a while before delivering his verdict. The local doctor, who wrote much about Stevens in his diary, concluded that this particular wizard was a highly intelligent man who used his knowledge of human nature and of his neighbours to solve the various problems brought before him.

One pellar who lived at St Erth in the 1860s was widely credited with saving the life of a jobbing workman. The man was repairing a house roof when he slipped and fell, hitting his head hard as he landed on the ground. The unconscious man had his head bandaged and was hurriedly lifted into a cart to be carried off to the nearest doctor. As the cart trundled past the home of the pellar, the horses stopped of their own accord. The pellar stepped out and asked what was wrong. On being told, he laid his hands on the bandages covering the injury and muttered under his breath for some minutes. Then he stepped back and said 'He'll be right now.' The workman recovered his senses a few seconds later and, when the bandages were removed, there was no sign of bleeding and only a small scratch to be seen.

This gift of staunching bleeding was one of the most useful in the armoury of the Cornish pellar, and one of the most used. A doctor newly arrived in Penzance wrote to a friend in 1913 that 'miners not infrequently come to my practice with wounds which by all appearance should have made them weak from loss of blood. On questioning them, however, they admit having been in the first place to a charmer, who had staunched the bleeding so effectually that all that they subsequently required of me was that the wounds should be dressed to make them heal more quickly'.

Perhaps there is something in the power of witches after all.

CHAPTER 9

MYSTERIOUS BEASTS

The B3254 from Liskeard to Launceston is a pretty road, popular with the motoring tourists who come to Cornwall for just such picturesque drives. Some of those tourists might see more than they expected, for this is the home of Carrier, one of the more active of the many lane dogs of Cornwall.

Carrier is typical of the lane dogs. It is big, black and sinister. It is seen loping along the road oblivious to everything in its path. It takes as little notice of modern cars and lorries as it did of horsemen and coaches in days gone by. Drivers have been forced to swerve out of its way to avoid colliding with this great dog with shaggy hair and staring eyes. Carrier's single-minded pursuit of his journey is all that counts. Unless, that is, somebody is foolish enough to block his path.

If Carrier is stopped from following his ever-repeating journey up the B3254 he becomes angry. Stopping in his tracks, the dog snarls maliciously. His eyes glow a fearsome red – like hot coals it is said. In most instances this has persuaded the person blocking the path to get out of the way, but the damage has been done. Bad luck will inevitably come to the person who dared to cross Carrier.

The B3254 from Liskeard to Launceston is haunted by Carrier, the lane dog.

Carrier is seen more at Berriowbridge than at any other spot along the road.

Carrier is seen more at Berriowbridge than at any other spot along the road. He comes down the hill from Middlewood at a steady run and lopes over the bridge before continuing up the hill the other side towards Launceston. Descending from the south-west corner of the bridge is a narrow flight of stone steps, now much overgrown. These lead down to a small pool of water beside the river. No doubt it was built so that travellers could drink or fetch water for their horse on hot days. Today it provides an eerie perch from which to watch the road.

It is interesting that Carrier should frequent this spot. The river which the bridge spans is the Lynher. Some miles downstream on the Lynher is St Germans, the site of one of Cornwall's most famous hauntings. This is where Dando and his pack of hell-hounds ride in search of the souls of the damned. Perhaps there is something about the waters of the Lynher that make it attractive to mysterious dogs.

Having crossed this river, Carrier continues on to Launceston where – according to one version of the story – he vanishes outside the mediaeval church of St Mary Magdalene.

Another lane dog, this time called Darley, frequents North Hill on Bodmin Moor. Unlike Carrier, Darley is a small white dog which can turn black and swell up to the size of a calf when angry. The road outside the church of St Blaise in St Blazey is the route taken by a great black dog. This hound seems to have been linked in some way to the stocks in which criminals were chained. The stocks now stand inside the church, a fine structure of 1445 elegantly restored by Edmund Sedding in 1897. In years gone by, however, the stocks stood outside, between the church and the neighbouring pub. Perhaps the dog had an affinity for wrong-doers.

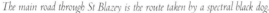

The main road through St Blazey is the route taken by a spectral black dog.

Yet another lane dog runs from Upton Cross to Stoke Climsland via Linkinhorne. Often seen at the ford in a narrow lane near Stoke Climsland is a giant black dog with blazing red eyes the size of saucers. A legend recorded in the 1880s said that the dog was, in fact, the ghost of a miner killed at Marke Valley Mine. More usually it is said to be an evil spirit. Either way, it is wise not to get in its path.

Another mysterious dog features in a letter written in 1860s by a doctor in Looe to a relative:

'Some weeks past a young boy of the town came me with a small wound to his hand. It looked as if he had been bitten by a small dog or a fox. The lad told a most curious tale. He had encountered a small dog with big eyes on the cliffs west of the town when out after seabird eggs. The dog lay still as he approached and the lad thought it tame, but it then bit him and ran off.

'The wound was not deep, so I applied the usual ointments and bound it up. Some days after the boy returned with his father. The small wound had turned gangrenous. I had no choice but to amputate. Sadly the boy died soon after.

'In itself this was most odd, for the wound was minor and I had hoped for recovery. But it was not long before I was told by old folk in town that my efforts had been in vain from the start. They said that the boy had met the Daisy Dog, which would seem to be a local superstition. This dog is said to be small and have long silky hair with a pug nose, needle-like teeth and a feathery tail. It guards treasure up on the cliffs and its bite is fatal.'

This Daisy Dog has cropped up in the folklore of south-east Cornwall in various guises over the years. It is invariably regarded with fear and dread.

These various lane dogs are almost certainly more closely linked to the supernatural than to anything that could be called real. Their appearance and habits are similar to those of other supernatural beasts, such as those linked in legend to fairies or witches. But not all the mysterious beasts reported in Cornwall can be dismissed so easily.

Take, for instance, the Wolf of Ludgvan. So far as can be deduced from historic records, the last wild wolf in England was killed in Cheshire in the 15th century. The last British wolf was the lone beast brought down by hunters in the Scottish highlands in 1743.

Despite this a wolf was active killing sheep near Ludgvan in the 1770s. Farmers who were losing livestock found the tracks of what they at first took to be a large dog. When one of them actually saw the culprit he declared it was a wolf. Not everyone believed him, but the sheep killings continued. Soon the locals had formed a group that organised watches to be kept. Then the wolf grew too bold and attacked a child. It was driven off by the would-be prey's playmates, but the incident sealed its fate.

The road from Upton Cross to Stoke Climsland is the home of a giant black dog with blazing red eyes the size of saucers.

Now it was not only a few farmers who wanted rid of the Ludgvan wolf, but all the locals. A great hunt was organised in which local gentry took part as well as the farmers, miners and others. The wolf was eventually cornered and killed at Rospeith Farm. Those who saw the body were in no doubt at all that it was a wolf, though the remains have unfortunately not been preserved for modern inspection.

Quite how a wolf could suddenly appear in an area where wolves had been extinct for some two centuries was never really explained. It has been suggested that the wolf must have escaped from somewhere. But this was long before the days of zoos, private or otherwise. The only wild animals that were kept captive were those that would perform – such as dancing bears – or which could be set to fight each other for entertainment. There is no record of a wolf ever being kept for either purpose.

Equally out of place in Cornwall is the more recent, and rather more notorious, Beast of Bodmin. This animal is generally thought to be a real creature, though there has never been any conclusive proof that it exists. The beast is usually described as being similar to a black panther or leopard. Certainly it is a very large cat-like animal.

The first hints that there might be something odd living up on Bodmin Moor came in the mid-1980s. Sheep farmers began to report that several partially eaten sheep had been found with their throats ripped out in a particularly violent and distinctive way. The way in which the throat wounds were inflicted convinced several of the farmers that the culprit was not a dog. Attacks on sheep by pet dogs allowed to run loose by irresponsible owners are unfortunately all too numerous and farmers are accustomed to seeing such injuries. These new attacks seemed to be something quite different.

After the sheep killings had been going on for some time, people began to report seeing a large cat-like creature moving about. By the early 1990s the Beast of Bodmin, as the mysterious creature had been dubbed, was widely known across Cornwall. It began to feature in local news media and by 1993 had hit the national headlines. In 1995 the British Government's Ministry of Agriculture had become sufficiently interested in the unexplained sheep killings that it funded an official investigation. The team of officials spoke to witnesses, studied casts of tracks and inspected the remains of dead sheep.

On 19 July 1995, after 26 days of work, the team delivered its findings to a meeting packed out with local farmers and national journalists. There was, the report concluded, no firm evidence to support the notion that big cats stalk Bodmin Moor in Cornwall. The wounds on the sheep were found to be consistent with kills by dogs, while the video footage and photographs which were claimed to show big cats on the moor were actually showing ordinary domestic cats.

Officially, the Beast of Bodmin did not exist. But not everybody was willing to accept the Ministry's version of events. Rosemary Rhodes, a farmer from near Bolventor, told journalists after the meeting that she had seen a black panther herself. 'Everybody in the country will think we have been suffering from some kind of mass hallucination,' she said. 'But one day, there is an outside chance somebody is going to get hurt. Every now and then I think I have imagined seeing the big cats but then I catch another glimpse and know I've been right all along.'

Richard and John Goodenough, farmers on Bodmin Moor for over 30 years, were equally adamant that they had lost 14 sheep to mystery killings. They claimed to have seen a black leopard four times.

The local MP Paul Tyler said: 'If the "Sherlock Holmes" team from the ministry think they have dispelled the mystery, I think they have another thing coming. A lot of people I meet and whose word I trust say "yes there is something there".'

Certainly the sightings of a Beast on Bodmin Moor continued. In 1997 the Royal Air Force decided to take a hand. RAF reserve volunteers camped in ditches and under hedges with the latest military night-vision equipment in an attempt to find evidence that the mystery big cat existed. Squadron Leader Andrew McCombe later reported that the intruder detection devices had been triggered several times, but that dense mist had made it impossible to be certain what was being detected. 'Something was moving along the tracks,' he said, 'but because of the cloud we could not get a good look.'

In August 1998 a 20-second video was released and was declared by some wild cat experts to be the best evidence yet that big cats roam Bodmin Moor. Others disagreed. The video footage was rather blurred and there was nothing in the frame that could be used to give a size for the cat-like creature that was shown.

Then a strange skull with large fangs was found on the banks of the Fowey on Bodmin Moor. The finder was a 14-year-old schoolboy, who took the skull home to his father. The father wondered if it could be the remains of the beast and sent it to the Natural History Museum in London for identification. The skull was quickly identified as being that of a leopard. The media speculation was quick, but doomed to disappointment. The skull showed unmistakable signs of having been prepared by a taxidermist, probably to form part of a leopard-skin rug. The skull had almost certainly been placed beside the footpath by a hoaxer hoping that it would be found and taken seriously.

The sheep killings and sightings continued. In 2003 a total of 96 sightings were reported, though not all of them were particularly convincing, even to those who take the Beast of Bodmin seriously. The beast remains the subject of much interest. In the autumn of 2007 the Cornish tourist attraction Colliford Lake Park held a 'Spookfest'. The highlight of the event was the burning of a 28ft tall wooden sculpture of the Beast of Bodmin Moor.

The Beast of Bodmin is not alone, however. Not far to the north-east, the bleak uplands of Exmoor are prowled by an equally elusive Beast of Exmoor. This is similarly described as being a large cat-like creature. Over the years there have been others such as the Surrey Puma, the Nottingham Lion and the Fen Tiger. To date the only one of these mysterious big cats whose existence has been proved beyond doubt was the Inverness Puma. This beast was reported for some weeks before it was captured by farmer Ted Noble on 29 October 1980. The puma, for it was undoubtedly of that species, was a healthy six-year-old animal. Its origin remains a mystery. This cat was named Felicity and spent the rest of her life at a local zoo. When she died her skin was stuffed and it is now on display in Inverness Museum.

The usual explanation given for the Beast of Bodmin, and indeed for other big cats, is that they are real animals that have escaped or been released from captivity. Until the Dangerous Animals Act of 1976 it was legal for people in Britain to keep almost any animal that they cared to have without a license or official supervision of any kind. Although it was not known how many big cats were kept by private individuals, there were certainly several dozen. When the 1976 Act became law most of those animals remained in private hands, though now under licence and in approved conditions. A few were handed over by people who did not want to upgrade their facilities to meet the new requirements. It has long been suspected that some big cats were released into the wild at this time by owners who did not want to hand their animals over to the Government. There is anecdotal evidence that up to 23 such cats may have been released.

At the end of the day, the mystery of the Beast of Bodmin remains unsolved. If the beast was an escaped black leopard, then it would have reached the end of its natural life some years ago. The fact that it continues to be seen into the 21st century would indicate that there is a small breeding population up on the moor. If this were so, however, there should be rather more evidence for their existence than has been found. This line of thought has led some researchers to suggest that the Beast of Bodmin has never actually been a real animal at all. They suggest that it is a phantom creature or ghost. They speculate that it may be linked to the various prehistoric religious sites on the moor.

Others think that there was originally a big cat on Bodmin, but that it did die some years ago. The sightings since then are explained as being due to simple misidentification. If a person sees a dog running wild at a distance or in poor light they might conclude that they have seen the beast simply because this is the first explanation that springs to mind. Sceptics, of course, suggest that there was never anything unusual up on Bodmin Moor at all. They say that the original sheep killings were most likely due to a big dog and that everything since has been produced from the imagination of people who had already heard of other alleged big cats elsewhere in Britain. Thus anything odd was explained in terms of a mystery big cat, when there was never any such creature.

The British Big Cats Society has been founded to identify scientifically, quantify, catalogue and protect the Big Cats that freely roam the British countryside. Perhaps one day the truth will be discovered. Animals that may be real, but for the existence of which there is no conclusive proof, are generally called cryptids, meaning 'hidden', and their study

The infamous Beast of Bodmin Moor is said to be a leopard or puma living wild on the bleak uplands.

is known as cryptozoology or the study of hidden animals. Cornwall is almost unique in Britain for having not just one cryptid, but two. In addition to the Beast of Bodmin, there is also the Morgawr.

The Morgawr has a longer history than the Beast of Bodmin, but it is not so well known outside Cornwall. Although stories of it date back centuries, the first documented encounter came in 1876 when fishermen in Gerrans Bay found a huge sea snake tangled in their nets. They prudently set it free. A similar serpent was spotted off Land's End in 1906.

The modern era of Morgawr sightings began in September 1975 at Pendennis Point. Mrs Scott and her friend Mr Riley saw what they described as a hideous, hump-backed creature, with stumpy horns, and bristles down the back of its long neck, swimming close off shore. The huge animal dived for a few seconds, then resurfaced with a conger eel in its jaws before diving again and disappearing from view. The report hit the local headlines. The newspapers were soon hearing from mackerel fishermen who blamed the strange beast for bad luck, bad weather and bad catches.

In February 1976 the *Falmouth Packet* published two photographs of Morgawr, taken by a lady who called herself 'Mary F'. They showed a long-necked, hump-backed creature. The photographer said that the creature had been black or very dark brown in colour and about 18ft long. She claimed to have sighted it swimming in the water off Trefusis Point. Unfortunately the photos were not very clear and did not constitute firm evidence.

Since then reports of Morgawr have continued to trickle in from locals and holiday-makers alike. The size of the beast has been estimated at anything from 12 to 45ft. The descriptions, however, remain consistent. The creature is said to have a small head and long neck, which is often held vertically out of the water. Behind the neck is a hump or humps that seem to constitute the body of the animal. There are no reports of an obvious tail, such as is seen when a whale or dolphin dives from view. Morgawr is seen most often off the mouth of the Helford River and around Falmouth Bay.

Whatever Morgawr is, the fact that it is seen in the sea would indicate that it is not a Cornwall-only creature. Indeed, similar sea animals have been widely reported over the years. In 1905 a pair of scientists, both Fellows of the Zoological Society, were on the yacht Valhalla off the coast of Brazil when they saw a creature neither could identify. It consisted of a small head on the end of a neck about 8ft long and as thick as a man's waist. Behind the neck was a hump 6ft long and 2ft tall. The creature was dark brown and moved forward slowly. The head was, the men thought, rather like that of a turtle. In 1848 a similar creature was seen by the officers of HMS *Daedalus* in the Atlantic.

Exactly what this sea creature might be is unknown. Given that a new species of whale was discovered as recently as the 1980s, it does not seem beyond belief that some type of large sea creature of unknown type might exist. Commander Rupert Gould of the Royal Navy undertook a wide ranging study of the evidence relating to the sea serpent after he retired. He concluded that although there was no incontrovertible evidence, there was enough to indicate that something was being seen by sailors. He thought it most likely to be a gigantic form of long-necked seal or long-necked turtle, but was wise enough to leave the final answer open.

There are certainly mysterious animals in and around Cornwall. It is to be hoped that they survive long enough for their existence to be proved beyond doubt.

CHAPTER 10

MYSTERIOUS SAINTS

More than any other part of Britain, Cornwall is a land of saints. Many of the villages and towns are named in honour of a patron saint, while springs and other natural features are named for saints by the dozen. What is most striking about these Cornish dedications is that they are very often to saints unknown elsewhere. While English churches are dedicated to St Michael, St Peter or St Paul, those in Cornwall are dedicated to local men and women for these are Cornish dedications to Cornish saints. Some of these Cornish holy figures are so utterly obscure that almost nothing is known about them. They are mysterious names from a mysterious time. Yet they were great and famous people in their day. By tracking down local legends and setting them against the bigger picture of British history it might be possible to form something of a picture of the time when saints walked in Cornwall.

Christianity came to Britain at least as early as 209, when a man named Alban was martyred in the town of Verulamium, now known as St Albans. The new religion made slow progress, though by 320 there were four bishops in Britain. We don't know where they were based – though one was almost certainly in London – but the religion was one of townsfolk that had not yet reached rural areas such as Cornwall.

In 429 the church in Britain split from that on the Continent. The secular government of Britain had left the Roman Empire 19 years earlier and that may have encouraged a more independent streak in the ecclesiastical authorities. The dispute erupted over the writings of the highly educated and much admired British monk Pelagius. As he grew older, Pelagius became more extreme. In 418 Pelagius was expelled from Rome by Pope Zosimus and his teachings condemned as heretical. Some of the finer points of Pelagianism can be obscure even to modern theologians, but the main thrust of his argument was clear enough. Pelagius argued that whether or not any particular human was to find salvation was a matter between that human and Christ. The human could help his cause through good works, charity and righteousness, but the final decision rested with God. Of more practical importance, Pelagius stated that priests should teach their fellow humans about God's grace and guide them along the right path, not act as intermediaries between humans and God. Still less was the Church to be a hierarchy of bishops and archbishops with a bureaucracy and wealth of its own. This was in direct conflict with the developing doctrine of Papal supremacy developing in Rome. Zosimus and his followers claimed that humans could find salvation only through the intermediary of the Church headed by the Pope.

The split between Britain and Rome prompted Bishop Germanus of Auxerre to travel to Britain. He preached against the Pelagian views, championed in Britain by Bishop Agricola. Although he gained a good deal of support for maintaining links with Rome, Germanus failed to enforce orthodoxy. Next the Pope sent his own deacon, Palladius, to Britain. The official mission of Palladius was to convert the Irish, but he put most effort into an attempt to suppress Pelagianism. He failed and died on his way back to Rome. His place as the head of the mission to the Irish was taken by the much more famous Patrick, a British Christian, who landed in Ireland in 432 and never left.

The last firm view that history has of the Christian Church in Britain comes in around 445 when Patrick got embroiled in a dispute with some unnamed bishops in Britain. The Christians then were a majority of the population, but they remained strongest in towns and urban areas. The bishops and priests were drawn from wealthy families who could afford the complex education in biblical and theological texts considered necessary. The Church itself owned a fair amount of property and land. Beyond this time all dates in British history for the next two centuries or so are speculative and may be as much as 30 or 40 years adrift of reality. Despite this, the sequence of events remains clear.

The writings of the monk Gildas survive from about the year 540. By that date things had changed dramatically. The central authority of post-Roman Britain had collapsed. In the west tribal princes held sway. Cornwall was part of the Kingdom of Dumnonia, ruled over by Prince Constantine. Lowland Britain was largely divided up between the civitas councils which had looked after local government in Roman times. These were now independent, some retaining a vestige of democratic structures and others under the sway of local tyrants. The new power in the land was the pagan English. When Gildas was writing the English had directly settled only in Kent and East Anglia, but they were launching raids and pillaging expeditions further west. Several of the petty civitas states had accepted a form of overlordship to English kings, paying them taxes and tribute.

The British Church had declined greatly. Most bishops and abbots were now appointed by the local secular ruler, and they were given their posts for political reasons, not on the basis of ecclesiastical virtue. Constantine of Dumnonia actually made himself an abbot so that he could harvest the rents of the monastery. Many bishops behaved no better than princes, and several owed allegiance to the pagan English. The number of Christians was in decline as the church hierarchy collapsed and paganism gained prestige with every English victory.

The work of reform began around the year 530, but gained pace only slowly. It was begun by a group of dedicated and austere monks in Wales. Samson, Illtud and David are the best known of these. Another was Paul Aurelian, the son of a Dumnonian landowner who had estates in Cornwall. Paul was educated in Wales, then set up a small monastery for like-minded Christians on some land given him by his father. About the year 555 Paul was invited by King Mark of Dumnonia to become chief bishop of the kingdom. Paul refused.

It was in the years that immediately followed Paul's refusal that Britain underwent the most profound changes. Most of Roman Britain fell to the English invaders. Not only were the political structures destroyed, but so was the ecclesiastical set up. Most Christians abandoned their faith as paganism established itself. Only a very few Christian communities survived.

In those areas that did not fall – Dumnonia was one – the Christian faith underwent a great change. Gone was the emphasis on urban congregations ruled by priests. Instead rural communities of monks and nuns became more common. These holy people led lives of the utmost austerity and sanctity. They believed that only by leading lives approved of by God could they save their own souls and lead their people to freedom from the rise of paganism. It was from this background that the Cornish saints sprang. The conversion of the rural population from paganism or a more lax version of Christianity began around the year 550 or so and took a couple of generations to complete. Most of the missionaries came from monasteries based in Dumnonia or Wales. Northern and western Cornwall were converted by missionaries from Ireland. One of the greatest of these missionary monks was St Petroc, now the patron saint of Cornwall. The hagiography, or saintly biography, of St Petroc was written many years after his death and contains much that is clearly fabulous. From this book, the survival of his name in placenames and Church dedications it is possible to put together a brief account of his work.

Petroc was the youngest son of Prince Glywys Cernyw, ruler of the petty state of Glywysing in southern Wales. As a young man Petroc, with some followers, left to study in Ireland. After several years of study, Petroc undertook a missionary journey to Cornwall. He landed in the estuary of the River Camel at a place called Llanwethinoc. He there established a monastery, and the place name changed to Petrocstow (meaning Petroc's place), which has since corrupted to Padstow. Petroc remained based at Padstow for the rest of his life, though he travelled widely through Dumnonia to found churches and monasteries. His name is preserved in five places in Cornwall and 13 in Devon. His most important foundation was the monastery of Bothmena (meaning the Place of Monks), now called Bodmin. He also travelled over the sea to Wales, founding at least the church in the village of St Petrox. He is said to have gone on a pilgrimage to Rome by way of Brittany, which is not impossible. His body was buried in Bodmin. Several of his bones were afterwards kept as relics in Bodmin. Although they were destroyed during the Reformation the ivory casket in which they were kept survives. Beyond that, the other stories about St Petroc are impossible to verify. It is highly unlikely that he went to India to live for seven years on an island accompanied only by a wolf. Assorted miracles ascribed to him are also told of other saints, and so are unlikely to be true.

Pinning down a date for St Petroc is very difficult. He is said to have met St Samson when he first arrived in Cornwall, which might place that event around 550. He is also said to have converted Prince Constantine of Dumnonia to Christianity some years later, but Constantine died in about 540. He is also said to have met St Guron, which would put his activities about the year 570. His death is traditionally said to have occurred in 564. Whatever the truth, St Petroc was clearly one of the earliest and most successful of the monk missionaries to convert the Cornish to the stricter sect of Christianity that came to hold sway over non-pagan areas of Britain by around 650.

Petroc was far from being alone in his work. We know even less about most of the missionaries than we do about St Petroc. The Irish monk St Ludewon, for instance, came to Cornwall in about the year 580. His name survives in that of the village of St Ludgvan. The church of St Ludgvan was completely rebuilt in 1336, sweeping away the earlier 10th-century church known to have stood there. In 1962 some repair work revealed that one of the stone stairs in the tower was a reused section of an upright preaching cross. The decorations were badly weathered but have been dated on stylistic grounds to the late sixth century. It might even be the original stone cross set up by St Ludewon from which to preach the gospel to the local pagans.

Another early saint, St Senara, gave her name to Zennor. St Senara was originally from Brittany, though she was educated in Ireland. The current church was begun in 1150, but is still dedicated to St Senara. The locals proudly tell the tale of a visiting lady from London who was travelling from St Ives to St Just by bus in the 1920s. As the bus rounded a corner, Zennor came into sight.

'My,' remarked the grand lady, 'what a quaint little village. But how small and how poor it is.'

The bus conductor, a native of Zennor, drew himself up proudly.

'Madam,' he replied as haughtily as he could, 'when London was but a collection of mud huts, Zennor was a church town.'

The conductor may be forgiven for some exaggeration, but his history was sound enough. St Senara has been dated to around 570 or so. She came to the location to found her Christian community as it was a fairly substantial village. At the same date, London was a pagan town. The English had abandoned the Roman city and were living a short distance to the west, around what is now Aldwych, where they could pull their flat-bottomed ships up on to a gravel bank. It was not until 596 that Pope Gregory I sent St Augustine to convert the English with orders to establish his diocese in London. Even then, St Augustine failed and had to settle for Canterbury instead. London remained defiantly pagan for another 50 years or so. The village of St Ewe is named for St Ywa who brought Christianity there and founded a nunnery at Lanua in around 580. St Ladock is named for the Irish woman missionary St Ladoca who came here with St Piran. St Piran moved on, but St Ladoca remained to preach to the locals. The ruins of what is thought to have been her little hut have been found beside a spring a short distance from the present church, begun around 1080.

St Senara, shown on the stained-glass window in her church at Zennor. St Senara was originally from Brittany but came to convert the pagans in Cornwall.

St Piran was, with St Petroc, one of the leaders of the missionary movement. He became the patron saint of tin miners and is regarded by some as the patron saint of Cornwall. His emblem of a white cross on a black field is now used as the unofficial flag of Cornwall. St Piran undoubtedly came to Cornwall from Ireland, but his actual origins are rather obscure. One version has it that he was the son of Dywel, a junior prince of the Dumnonian royal family, who went to Ireland to be educated. Another version states that he was born in Offaly of humble parents. Whatever the truth, he came to Cornwall somewhere between 540 and 560 to convert the locals. Having left St Ywa to her work, Piran travelled widely before settling down to found a monastery with himself as the first abbot. The place became known as Perranzabuloe in his honour. He died there in around 580 or so and his relics were preserved there until the Reformation, except for one arm, which was taken to Exeter Cathedral. He is said to have died on 5 March, now St Piran's Day.

Many legends gathered around St Piran. One is that he set tin smelting on to a sound business footing after the main tin trade to the Continent had been lost with the fall of the Roman Empire. He was supposed to have demonstrated one method of smelting tin by placing a large slab of black rock into a furnace and inducing the tin to float to the surface as a white cross – this being the origin of his symbol.

Another legend states that St Piran came to Cornwall by means of divine intervention. He had been intending to convert some pagan villages in southern Ireland, but the angry pagan priests had seized him. They tied Piran to a millstone and threw him into the sea. The millstone had miraculously floated to Cornwall, which Piran took to be a sign from God that he should do his work there. This legend of a floating millstone is told of several saints active around the Irish Sea at this time, and is thought to have origins in reality. The usual boat used for sea crossings to and from Ireland was the curragh. This was a boat made from a frame of springy tree branches covered over with sheets of leather, sewn together with leather thongs and then waterproofed with pitch. Each boat could carry a dozen men or so. The structure of the boats was strong, but light. They were habitually ballasted with piles of stones, but some carried a single millstone instead. This may have been the origin for the many stories of holy men, such as St Piran, floating about on millstones.

Another saint to come from Ireland was St Goran, after whom the village of Gorran is named. He may have originally been Welsh, but was educated in Ireland before reaching Cornwall. At first he went to the monastery at Bodmin, but St Petroc advised him to seek solitude and privacy where he could devote himself utterly to God. St Goran duly set off heading south, finding the place he sought a day's walk away. His sanctity attracted followers, despite his desire for solitude, and Gorran grew out of that community. The present church of St Goran was begun in around 1100 a few yards from his original cell, ruins of which remain. The church was rebuilt in around 1480 with a massive 100ft tall granite tower topped by a mighty steeple. For many years the steeple acted as a landmark for fishermen putting into Gorran Haven, but it fell down in 1606 and was never rebuilt.

St Mewan was a Welshman who went to Brittany to be educated in the Christian faith. He is said to have been distantly related to St Samson and to have stayed in a monastery founded by Samson for some years. He then travelled to Cornwall to find St Samson and to establish a Christian community a short distance from the home of his relative. That community became St Mewan, once a prosperous tin mining town but now a small rural hamlet. The name of Mewan may be a corruption of the family name Mevennus, which is known from some manuscript records from later Roman times in Gaul. One of the prime duties of these early missionaries was to baptise converts, usually standing as godfather to those they had converted. The duties of godfather in those days included ensuring that the converts received a sound education in the basics of the Christian faith. One of those to whom St Mewan stood godfather was Austol, who gave his name to St Austell. The church he founded in his new Christian town was, for some reason that has not survived, rededicated in the 15th century to the Holy Trinity. The church was entirely rebuilt and richly decorated with statues and carvings suitable to its new dedication. These survived the Reformation and make a visit to St Austell worthwhile for that reason alone.

One of the more enigmatic Cornish saints is St Crida the Virgin. She gave her name to the village of Creed, but very little is known about her. She may have been a contemporary of St Ywa, perhaps even a friend or colleague. The porch to her church has some wonderfully unusual carved stone heads of undoubtedly early but unknown date. Other Cornish saints are even more obscure, none more so than the St Dennis who has a church dedicated to him high on Goss Moor north-west of St Austell. This church dates to the 14th century, but the site is undoubtedly one of the very earliest Christian places in Cornwall. In the churchyard stands a preaching cross that has been dated to about the year 500. So little is known of St Dennis that it has been suggested that he is really St Denis, or Dionysus, who was the first bishop of Paris. This St Denis was martyred by being beheaded in about the year 250. He has no known links to Cornwall.

Another idea relates to the original use of the title of 'saint' in the British church. The title did not originally mean anything more than 'holy' or 'learned' and could be applied to almost any person who devoted themselves to a Christian lifestyle. The church of St Dennis is built within an old fortified hilltop. These earthworks topped by timber walls were known as 'dinas' in the old Celtic language. So the name of 'St Dennis' may be derived from 'Saint Dinas', meaning the holy hillfort. There never was a Cornish saint named Dennis at all.

Many of the Cornish saints gave their names to wells or springs. The old pagan Celtic religion that Christianity replaced also placed a strong faith in springs and wells, which were mostly sacred to female deities of local fame. It is more than likely that the missionaries rededicated sacred pagan springs to the Christian God so that the locals could continue with their popular customs in the name of the new God. One of the few places to preserve a trace of this pagan origin is the Spring of Colurion just outside Ludgvan. Colurion is an undoubtedly Celtic name and in no known text is a Christian saint of this name recorded. To make the ancient link even clearer, a local legend has it that the waters were 'sacred before the saints came'.

One of the most famous of these holy springs is the well of St Madron, or Madern, near Penzance. On Wednesdays in May this well had the power to cure almost any skin ailment. The ritual bathing involved the person, wearing only a shirt, walking through the pool of water by the spring three times, turning counterclockwise, then emerging to walk around the pool seven times clockwise. A strip of cloth then had to be torn from the shirt and left hanging on a nearby tree. All this had to be carried out in absolute silence. The nearby Doom Well was supposed to show a vision of the future if a bent pin were dropped into it. The Doom Well was filled in during the 1930s. Still open is the Holy Well at Roche, which also demanded a sacrifice of a bent pin if it were to work. This well was powerful only at dawn on Maundy Thursday. The bent pin had to be tossed in by an unmarried woman so that it caused bubbles to form. The woman could then stare at the bubbles to see into her future.

Rather more impressive were the properties of St Nun's Well at Altarnon. This was supposed to cure of insanity anyone who bathed in it naked. The Holy Well, or Scarlet's Well, at Bodmin gives forth waters that contain an oily scum on the surface. In bright daylight this oil produces a rainbow glitter of iridescent colours. It was long thought to be able to alleviate all sorts of aches and pains. At Callington the Dupath Well, now covered by a small mediaeval stone shrine, was said to give waters that could cure whooping cough. The well at Rock had similar powers. The holy well of St Cuby at Duloe gives forth waters of great, but unspecified power. St Cuby is unknown anywhere other than at this well. He is often said to be identical to St Cuthbert. That saint, however, was active in northern England between 660 and 687 and is not known ever to have got further south than the River Trent at Nottingham. A more likely candidate is St Kybi, an Irish monk who visited Rome in around 468 after being expelled from a monastery on the Isle of Arran. He has no known links to Cornwall, but his name is similar and he was at least travelling around this part of Britain. The holy well of Holywell Bay is also dedicated to this enigmatic St Cuby. The spring is located in one of the various caves that open off the beach. Its waters are said to be able to cure dandruff and itchy scalps.

At Luxulyan there is a spring dedicated to St Cyr. It is covered over by a mediaeval shrine and at that time was a recognised centre of pilgrimage. This St Cyr was a local Cornishman who was one of the very first locals to embrace the Christian faith. He used this well, which stood on his farm, as a sacred font in which to baptise those whom he converted to the new faith. At some point the dedication of the adjacent church was changed from the local St

The holy well of Holywell Bay is located in the caves that line the cliffs facing the beach.

This 500-year-old baptistry at Luxulyan houses a spring dedicated to St Cyr.

Cyr to the very foreign St Cyriacus and his mother St Julitta. This holy pair lived in Iconium in Syria, but in 304 they fled to Tarsus to avoid persecution by the Roman Prefect Alexander. A short while later Alexander himself went to Tarsus, where he was told of Julitta and her son, who were newly arrived from his province. Alexander was suspicious and had them arrested in case Julitta was a criminal fleeing justice. When the pair were dragged in front of Alexander, Julitta refused to talk. The prefect then picked up the four-year-old Cyriacus and put on an act of being a kindly old uncle figure. When he asked Cyriacus why he and his mother had come to Tarsus, the boy replied 'Because I am a Christian and so is my mother.' Alexander threw the boy down, killing him as his head hit the stone floor. Julitta was subsequently tortured to death after refusing to renounce her faith.

Presumably some past vicar felt that his church needed a bit of classical glamour and so fixed on St Cyriacus because his name was similar to that of the local St Cyr. At least the old well retains the name of the original local saint.

Colan has two holy wells. The first is sacred to Our Lady of Nantes, the second to St Pedyr. Redruth has a spring dedicated, unsurprisingly, to St Ruth. This St Ruth was a local girl who habitually wore a red cloak, hence the name of her town. For some reason it is said that a child baptised in waters from this well can never be hanged by a rope. The well at St Cleer cured lunatics and, for some unexplained reason, it was forbidden to kill spiders near it. The spring at St Clethr gave waters that were generally good for health and well being.

Down the appropriately named Well Lane in Liskeard is to be found St Martin's Well. Engaged couples had to come to this well the day before their wedding. While holding hands they had to stoop down to collect a cup of water and share it. This, it was said, would ensure that the marriage would produce a good number of children. There are two candidates for the honour of being the St Martin in question, though it is a mystery as to why either would be considered a suitable fertility figure. The first was the governor of Britain in the year 353. When the Emperor Constantius ordered a persecution in Britain, Martin objected and was promptly put to death.

The second, and altogether more likely, candidate is St Martin of Tours. St Martin was Bishop of Tours in Gaul in the later 4th century. He never came to Britain, but his follower Victricius of Rouen did travel here in about 396. There is some reason to think that Victricius was himself British. At any rate he spread the teachings of St Martin, who championed the concepts of charity and good works over abstract theology. Pelagius counted himself a follower of the message spread by Victricius.

St Levan, named for a local missionary, has the Parchaple Well. St Levan was sitting near here fishing on Sunday afternoon when a woman named Joanna came by and reprimanded the saint for fishing on the Sabbath. Thereafter, any child named Joanna baptised with water from the well would, it was thought, grow up to be a fool. The name was traditionally never used in the village. Another holy well formerly stood beside the churchyard at Phillack.

Liskeard's St Martin's Well is said to ensure fertility to newly married couples.

It was desecrated in 1723 when a man named Erasmus Pascoe used it to wash his sheep on the way to market. The spring dried up and, as a result of his actions, Pascoe was dogged by bad luck all his life. The Pascoes were a wealthy local family and many of their graves lie in the churchyard, though the truth of the legend is uncertain to say the least.

Polperro has a holy spring which, if visited on three consecutive days at dawn, would cure sore eyes. St Breward's Well at St Breward was similarly good for eyes, but only if bent pins were thrown into the waters. Bent pins should also be thrown into the Menacuddle Well near St Austell on the road to Bodmin. Ulcers would be cured if the pins were offered correctly. St Genny's Well outside Launceston was vaguely sacred, as were St Ruan's well near Cadgwith and St Euny's holy well at Sancreed.

The church of St Anthony-in-Meneage was founded early in the Middle Ages when a group of Norman nobles were caught in a terrible storm when sailing to England. As the tempest reached its height, the nobles swore to found a church to St Anthony, patron saint of sailors, wherever they came safely to land. They landed here, near the mouth of the Helford River, and so paid for the construction of this church. St Germoe was an Irish king who was converted by St Patrick. He promptly gave up his throne and came over the sea with his sister Breage to live as a hermit. The pair landed at the mouth of the Hayle, then walked inland to reach Tregonning Hill, then a small village inside the ancient earthworks. Breage chose to stay in the village and subsequently found fame as a midwife.

Germoe wanted more solitude so he left to live beside a spring where St Germoe's Church was later built and the village of that name sprang up. Throughout the Middle Ages the tomb of St Germoe was a centre of pilgrimage, attracting visitors from across the south-west. The tomb was smashed at the Reformation, but the equally venerated St Germoe's Chair was left intact. The original spring was boxed in by granite slabs in 1977 and stands just outside the churchyard.

Another spring to have been recently restored is that of St Keyne, restored in 1976. It was long held to have the power to give supremacy in a marriage to whichever of the happy couple was the first to drink of its waters. The poet Robert Southey knew the legend and penned the lines

'I hastened as soon as the wedding was done
And left my wife in the porch;
But in faith she had been wiser than me
For she took a bottle to church.'

St Keyne herself was another Welsh missionary who came to convert the Cornish. She was the 15th of 26 children born to Prince Brechan of South Wales. She spent her adult life wandering around western Britain performing various miracles and converting local pagans. She died here, and with her dying breath blessed the spring waters.

St Keverne may have been a holy missionary, but he is said to have had a savage temper. When he first arrived on the Lizard Peninsula to found the village that bears his name, the locals treated him with outright hostility. In revenge Keverne declared that no metal would ring within the sounds of his bells. That is why, locals believed, no tin ore was to be found in the area. Once established, St Keverne invited St Just over to visit. St Just, it is said, noticed that St Keverne had a richly jewelled golden goblet that he used for holy communion. St Just wanted it for himself and stole it just before setting off home. Keverne gave chase when he noticed his loss and an unseemly fight took place between the two saints up on Crousa Down. Keverne got his chalice back safely. Keverne was rather better disposed to animals. One spring day as he was praying a pair of birds built a nest in a fold of his robes. St Keverne refused to move until the chicks had hatched for fear of harming one of God's creatures.

Another bad-tempered saint has a chair at St Mawes. St Mawes was sitting here preaching one day when a seal interrupted him by continually barking on the shore. In a fit of anger, St Mawes threw a rock which killed the hapless seal. St Nectan was a Welsh monk who came to Devon to live at Hartland. When he was an old man, St Nectan was annoyed by missionaries from the Pope in Rome. The Roman Church had a different way of calculating Easter from the native British church, and they wanted St Nectan to stop celebrating Easter when he believed the day fell and instead follow the orders of the Pope. In order to get some peace in his final years, St Nectan left Hartland and came to live beside a waterfall north of Bodmin Moor at what is now known as St Nectan's Kieve. When he felt death coming upon him, St Nectan threw his valuable chalice, platter and other plate into the pool at the foot of the waterfall, together with his silver bell.

'That bell will never ring again,' he said, 'until the true faith is restored to these islands.' He then ordered that his body should be buried beside the waterfall, and died.

In the 16th century a group of local tin miners decided to try to recover the allegedly fabulous treasure from the deep pool. As they prepared to dive in, they heard the soft tinkle of a silver bell, followed by a booming voice that declared 'The child is not yet born that shall get my treasure.' They wisely gave up the venture. The treasure is there still.

INDEX OF PLACE NAMES

ND - #0297 - 270225 - C0 - 234/156/12 - PB - 9781780913063 - Gloss Lamination